Robert McQueen Grant

October 17. '540

From F.

THE SERMON
ON THE MOUNT

The Sermon on the Mount

BY

MARTIN DIBELIUS

New York

CHARLES SCRIBNER'S SONS

MCMXL

FOREWORD

In the early months of the year 1937 Professor Martin Dibelius of the University of Heidelberg, Germany, delivered the John C. Shaffer Lectures at the Divinity School of Yale University. Returned to Germany he revised the manuscript for publication in book form, but circumstances prevented its reaching America for many months. The march of time since his revision would probably make him wish to revise still further the sections dealing with contemporary life. But as the larger part of the work concerns the historical interpretation of the Sermon on the Mount it has seemed feasible to publish the text virtually as he revised it in 1937, with only such minor, stylistic changes as I have found it necessary to make in reading proof.

During the course of his stay in America Professor Dibelius visited many of the Universities and Theological Seminaries of the United States as lecturer. To those with whom he came into contact in the course of these visits, this volume will serve as a pleasant reminder of his genial presence and as a token of his

cautious scholarship and his keen interest in the problems of Christianity. To all students of the New
Testament it provides a significant contribution to the
literature of the subject and a welcome addition to
the list of his publications available in the English
language.

CARL H. KRAELING

Yale University
June 21, 1940

CONTENTS

THE SERMON
ON THE MOUNT

CHAPTER I

Christianity and the Sermon on the Mount

CHRISTIANITY hås been embroiled in many conflicts during the nineteen centuries of its history, but that through which it is now passing is of a special character and of a special intensity. There is not merely, as there was in the past, a scientific criticism of Christianity coming from the side of natural science and questioning the incarnation as well as the resurrection of Christ and the miracle-stories of the Bible. There are not only, as in the past, historical questions concerning the life of Jesus and the originality of his message. There are not only, again as in the past, philosophical considerations which state that Christian ideals are not the highest in the world and that other ideals may be more helpful for the people of today and more suitable for human conduct in the modern world. All these kinds of antagonisms are still in existence, but the crisis of today involves a far greater issue. It is the Christian religion as a whole which is questioned, and not only questioned but actually attacked along the entire front.

For several decades past many men have been living practically outside of the realm in which the Gospel is officially preached, *i.e.*, the realm of the

Church. This indifference towards the Church has varied in degree according to the country. It was in most cases not an outspoken antipathy which separated men from the Church, but rather the conviction that the message or the help of the Church was not necessary for the individual. It was, in a word, the spiritual autarchy of modern man which prevented him from coming in touch with the Church. Actually in the hearts of these people who were by no means devoted to the Church there was often a deep respect for the message of the Church and for the Gospel; consequently they differentiated between the official representation of the Christian religion in the world and the personal appeal of the Gospel. They spoke about Christianity as an unmusical man would speak about music. This still holds good for many laymen today in Europe as well as in America.

In the meantime there arose a new and strong antagonism against Christianity, especially in the younger generation. It was new, for it was a result of the two great defeats of the Christian religion in modern times: Christianity's failure to prevent war with its hatreds, its horrors, its devastations and its unsatisfactory "peace" treaties, and Christianity's failure to contribute effectively to the solution of the social problem. This is the reason why many of our contemporaries lost all confidence in the forces of the Christian religion. Disappointed by all kinds of Christian leadership, they began to look for other ideals. In consequence of this antagonism against

Christianity our generation is faced with a new and great problem. This is expressed in the question whether the Christian message may still be regarded, as it was formerly, as the rule of conduct for mankind or at least for the civilized nations of the world —and if not, where the man of today can find such a rule.

In reply to this question some of our contemporaries probably would boast of their own respective philosophies of life. But it is not enough that certain educated men have a philosophical standard for their private lives. The rank and file have no philosophy at all; they need an authoritative message for family life, for commercial life, for political life, a message which is applicable to the requirements of this troubled time. Such a message should answer the questions of the man on the street as well as those confronting the governor of a state or the manager of a factory or the scholar in his study. Such a message, it is true, would not present a detailed ideal of individual or social life, for those ideals change in the course of centuries and differ according to different nations and races and continents. The message which we need would none the less be a dominant voice in the struggle for life, a powerful commanding force motivating our actions, a star illuminating our way, and in its possession we should be like the wise men from the East who, "when they saw the star, rejoiced with exceeding great joy."

The Christian Gospel was such a message in the

Middle Ages and continued to function as a norm through the Christian era until the seventeenth century, for the Christian section of mankind. It is an historical fact, however, that Christianity has lost this position. This has happened since the period of rationalism which was, in spite of its enormous advances in philosophical and scientific fields, the beginning of the secularization, *i.e.*, the unconscious neglect, of all supernatural obligations. It is an historical fact, too, that since the mechanization of modern life, since the great alteration of our civilization by machines, new values have become important for mankind and have overshadowed the old norm of Christian life. It is other rules which mankind follows in these days, and because the rules which attempt to guide humanity are not only other, but manifold and different, *guidance for humanity as a whole is entirely lacking*. Thus we are faced not only by a crisis in the Christian religion, but rather by a crisis in all the standards of human life.

However, Christians have never given way to despair. In the midst of all this trouble they have been compelled to consider what the meaning of Christianity was and is. To have a Christian faith today means to be convinced that, in spite of everything, the Christian message actually has redeeming force and significance for mankind. We acknowledge that the reason for the defeat of Christianity in the past was our own insufficiency. If anything, we are inclined to feel that the Christian message has not yet been fully interpreted, that the treasure of the Gospel has not yet been exhausted, because in the past the spirit of the age has exercised too much influence upon the preaching of the Gospel. Therefore, it ought to be the duty of Christians even today to preach by words or deeds not a so-called Christian ideal—which might only be a mixture of biblical and secular thought—but to preach the Gospel, the message of the New Testament.

It is rather hard to give a trustworthy and universally valid interpretation of the Christian religion. There are too many conceptions of the Christian faith, or at least too many different emphases upon individual aspects of the same faith. But the only trustworthy way to answer that question—namely what the true character of Christian religion is—is for every student of Protestant Theology to go back to the New Testament and refresh his understanding of the thought world of this small book. Of course, since the time of the New Testament writers, theological opinions and points of view have frequently changed; but Christian theology of the Protestant type takes and should take the New Testament as a standard.

Within this New Testament the Sermon on the Mount assumes the foremost position. It is one of the most characteristic documents, one of the most comprehensive expressions of the Christian attitude in the world and therefore most frequently subject to attack. Everybody who suffers for Christ comforts himself by the blessings of the Sermon on the Mount. But every opponent of the Christian faith also attacks the passage of the Sermon on the Mount: "I say unto you that ye resist not evil; but whosoever shall smite thee on the right cheek, turn to him the other also." The Sermon on the Mount is the great symbol of the Christian way of living, the weightiest evidence of Christian ethics. Therefore, since the task of Christian theology is to understand and to make clear the contents of the divine message revealed by Jesus Christ, the Sermon on the Mount must be studied again and again with the help of theological scholarship.

Consequently, the great problem which I posed at the beginning, namely, whether the Gospel of Jesus Christ is still a message to the world of today, is at the same time the problem of the Sermon on the Mount. It does not suffice to solve this problem by a general justification and recommendation of some isolated sayings of Jesus. We must go deeper. We must consider the origin and character of the entire section Matthew 5–7, the authenticity and meaning of its several sayings, the contents of the whole, its claims and its ultimate relation to human ideals. From this angle an inquiry into the Sermon on the Mount would at the same time provide an example of methodical New Testament exegesis.

For a methodical interpretation of New Testament texts the most important thing is a sound *philological approach*. By that I mean the ability to read and to understand what is written irrespective of personal opinion and prepossession. Theologians have often overlooked the importance of this requirement. They must realize that they owe to the word of the New Testament a strict philological treatment of the text. Where it is lacking, theological exegesis is open to the influence of all kinds of religious enthusiasts who discover in the Bible what they want to read. In the case of the Sermon on the Mount the philologist first asks himself what is the meaning of this section as it stands in Matthew. He differentiates between the work of the Evangelist and the material which the Evangelist received out of the earlier tradition. He considers the origin of this earlier tradition and its connection with those who were witnesses of the life of Jesus.

Here the purely philological questions resolve themselves into, and become part of, larger historical problems. We want to know which of these sayings are the authentic words of Jesus himself and what their meaning was in the original context in which they were spoken. Thus we face the great problem whether our knowlege of Jesus is and can be reliable. Perhaps the advances made in historical method in our time allow us to answer these questions in another way than former generations did. We have at our disposal new techniques of linguistic investigation, new approaches to literary problems, new archæological materials for a knowledge of the ancient East. We know better than other generations did the peculiarities of the Hellenistic Greek, the language of the

Mediterranean world since the days of Alexander the Great. We have investigated the origin of popular literature. Therefore we no longer treat the Gospels as if they were poetical or philosophical writings. We know better than before the background of Jesus' deeds as well as of Paul's mission. The more we are convinced that we have new knowledge and new materials, the greater is our obligation to apply them in an objective, disinterested way to the interpretation of the New Testament.

Only when the duties of the philologist and the historian have been fulfilled are we in a position to put the theological question in a strict sense.

The purpose of the evangelists in the composition of their Gospels was not merely to preserve the words of our Lord. In addition they handed down records of his deeds, they told the story of his Passion. When they did so, it was their task, as Luke says, to give to the Christian people of their generation "the certainty of those things wherein they have been instructed." To present historical evidence of the message they preached—this was their principal purpose. But the contents of this message was not only the admonition to love one's enemies, to pray the Lord's prayer, not to take thought for one's life and not to judge. It also embraced, among its most important elements, the Passion-Story with its christological bearing, interpreted "according to the Scriptures," the christological message as a whole and the eschatological message in addition. That Christ came from heaven to bring salvation for mankind and will come again in the near future to bring full redemption for the whole world in his Kingdom—this was the burden and the scope of the early Christian Evangel.

The very first glance seems to indicate that the Sermon on the Mount has nothing to do with this larger message of the Incarnation, Salvation and Redemption. And the farther it is from the larger Christian message, the nearer it is to the Wisdom Literature of the Jews. The sayings of the Prophets, of the Old Testament Poets and of the Jewish Rabbis have more resemblance to the words of the Sermon on the Mount than, let us say, the Pauline epistles. We are therefore obliged to ask what the reason for this difference may be. If the Sermon on the Mount does not concern the message of the Incarnation and Redemption, we must ask what its actual importance for the early Christian preaching may have been. We are not allowed to answer that it has no importance at all; for the fact that the Sermon on the Mount was handed down and put into writing gives strong evidence that it was important for preaching. The whole of the early Christian tradition, its formation and its perpetuation, is influenced by the requirements of preaching. In the Christian beginnings, when the communities were waiting for the end of the world and did not reckon with Christian generations after their own generation they preserved only material, oral or written, which they used for missionary preaching or for edification and education. For this reason, there must be some kind of unity between the Sermon on the Mount and the christological message in spite of first impressions.

To understand this problem is to find ourselves and all commentators of the Sermon on the Mount confronted with a new task. We must consider our text in the light of this supposed unity. Now the Sermon on the Mount belongs to the first half of the New Testament. It belongs to the life of Jesus, to the record of his acts among his people, to the story of his conflicts with the Pharisees and Scribes. It shows us the Lord sitting and teaching. But the very first readers of the Sermon on the Mount were themselves already Christians and their faith was not a faith merely in a teacher but in a Saviour and Redeemer. They understood Jesus' sermon not as wisdom, like the wisdom of the Old Testament teachers, but as revelation, not as the address of a Rabbi but as a message from God.

As the Church did, so we must combine the tradition of Jesus' words and deeds with the message of Christ's mission on earth. Only in this way we may hope to reach the understanding of the Sermon on the Mount which existed in the minds and souls of the first readers. It is the first task of a full theological interpretation to tell the modern reader what the first readers thought when they read this document of the Sermon on the Mount. Only if we bear this in mind are we protected against the influence of modern doctrines.

For a fruitful interpretation, however, it does not suffice to know the thoughts of the first readers. We must consider ourselves. Are we still in a position to understand and to carry out the Sermon on the Mount as a message of God? The conditions of life today are by no means what they were at the beginning of our era. The position of the Church has also changed in a remarkable way: the Church of to-day is more or less responsible for the attitude of millions of Christian people and in this way for conditions and institutions existing in a so-called Christian world. It may be questioned, and it must be questioned, whether the ideal of the Sermon on the Mount is still practicable for us, and, if so, why our life is so far from this ideal. And if the sayings and commandments pronounced in the days of old in Palestine are meaningless for our life and for our day, what shall we say about our claim to be Christians?

The great trouble today is that the world does not take Christianity seriously; and when the world of today refuses to take Christianity seriously it usually points to the difference between the actual Christian attitude and the message of the Gospel, especially the message of the Sermon on the Mount. If we really want to be honest, we must confess that the world is right in pointing to this discrepancy. We speak of the high Christian ideals of reverence to God and of love for one's neighbour. But the world does not see the effect, for the effect is too small. So it is the constant accusation of the world against Christendom that the

attitude of the Christians is not the attitude of a redeemed people.

This is the direction from which the great German
thinker, Friedrich Nietzsche, himself the son of a
German pastor, continually launched his attacks upon
Christianity. He wrote about the Christians in his
Zarathustra. "They should sing better hymns, then I
would believe in their Redeemer; his disciples should
look more like redeemed people." In these days when
some of Nietzsche's ideas are playing so important a
role in modern German thought, such accusations are
again very current, particularly among those of the
younger generation. Under these conditions our interpretation of the Sermon on the Mount cannot but become a kind of test. It will show us what we ought to
be and what we actually are.

To object that this is not a matter of scientific research would be incorrect, for the Sermon on the
Mount is not like a dead stone or a fossil. It is a text
which purports to be a living word. If its efficacy is not
recognizable in the world, we have to choose between
two explanations. Either its time has gone and the
Sermon on the Mount is a document of the past—and
nothing more. Or—and this is the second explanation
—its time will come and we are not yet in the right
position to be true Christians. This is, as I feel, the
greatest problem which the interpretation of the Sermon on the Mount puts before us.

CHAPTER II

The Character of the Sermon on the Mount

WE BEGIN our study of the Sermon on the Mount, Matthew 5–7, with the question most immediately suggested by the text as we read it, and ask what was the purpose of the Evangelist when he composed it and assigned it to its familiar place in his Gospel. As everybody knows, the materials contained in the Gospel of Matthew are not arranged in chronological order, and modern New Testament scholars have come more and more to the conclusion that the first communities were not interested in chronology at all. That is by no means an astonishing fact, for the first Christians needed not a biography of Jesus with chronological remarks but rather a collection of striking words by him and facts about him usable in the proclamation of the Kingdom of Heaven. Of course, when they collected sayings or incidents, they put them in a certain order. Apparently, the only order of the events in the life of Jesus which came down to the later evangelists was the order of Mark, and even this order was not an order in a strict chronological sense. Papias, the first author with literary interests in the ancient Church, recognized this on the ground of arguments which were apparently convincing for him, but which are unknown to us.

Consequently, we must conclude that all original knowledge of the historical order of events in the life of Jesus was lost in the early communities. For Luke, who, according to his introduction, would appear to be recording the events of Jesus' life "in order," is actually dependent upon the sequence of events which we read in Mark also. Certainly Luke has some special chronological presuppositions, for instance when he puts the story of the preaching at Nazareth at the beginning of Jesus' career. But these changes of order depend more upon the writer's own feeling than upon any tradition handed down to him. In the case of Matthew at least the second half of his Gospel gives clear evidence that the order of Mark underlies the course of his own story, and in the first half of his work he renounces chronology in favour of a systematic order of presentation. After the baptism and the temptation, the two introductory scenes, he relates only the calling of the disciples which is the indispensable beginning of Jesus' work, and then gives a general description of his preaching and healing in three verses, Matthew 4:23–25. What follows is a well-arranged section comprising five blocks of material. Since we do not find an analogous disposition of material elsewhere in the Gospels, we may conclude that the disposition in Matthew is created by the Evangelist himself. This is the sequence of his five blocks of material: first, words of Jesus (Sermon on the Mount, Matt. 5–7); second, Jesus' mighty works (8:1–9:34); third, Jesus' charge to his disciples (9:35–11:1); fourth, Jesus and his opponents (11:2–12:50); fifth, Jesus' teaching in parables (13:1–52). Three of these blocks may be called discourses, and of them the Sermon on the Mount is the first.

All these discourses—the Sermon on the Mount, the charge to the disciples and the teaching in parables—are compilations of individual sayings and groups of sayings. The question of the occasions at which Jesus spoke these several sayings we are not able to answer because the Evangelist does not tell us. That the Sermon on the Mount is not a real discourse the nature of its elements clearly demonstrates. They are mostly individual sayings brought together to form separate groups, *e.g.*, the beatitudes, the new commandments and the parables of the builders. Each group is complete in itself and has no visible connection with the other groups. Indeed, it is necessary to suppose that the different groups were addressed to *different hearers* and, consequently, were spoken at *different occasions*. Luke has reproduced most of these groups, though in a somewhat different setting. All so-called discourses in Matthew are composed in the same way, and this indicates that they are not real speeches. We may compare the speeches in the Acts of Apostles, the speeches of Peter, of Stephen, of Paul, if we wish to see what a real speech looks like. There the whole address treats a general theme which is dominant from the beginning to the end. There, but not in Matthew, we have before us genuine speeches, *i.e.*, genuine in style; the question of their historical reliability may be put aside in this connection.

Let me add to this philological statement concerning the different entities in the Sermon on the Mount a psychological observation. It is impossible to preach as Matthew shows Jesus preaching, for example, in his seventh chapter, where he presents a mass of single sentences without a common theme. If you were to read this chapter aloud, saying after saying, every word would overshadow the next, and no single saying would make its due impression on the listeners. It would take only six minutes to recite this seventh chapter of Matthew in the Greek wording, but listeners not acquainted with the content would find the speaker saying too much in too short a compass. It is quite clear that Jesus did not speak in this way, and that he spoke these various words at a variety of occasions. Therefore from this point of view the Sermon on the Mount is to be considered as a composite of sayings.

The fact that Matthew has placed this particular composite in the most prominent place in his book is of significance; he means it to give us no less than a general summary of Jesus' teaching. Before narrating the incidents of Jesus' career he wants to present Jesus' message by giving characteristic groups of his sayings. The Sermon on the Mount thus has a programmatic character. It is programmatic first of all for the record of Jesus' life and work providing the best example of his teaching, an impressive illustration of his manner of addressing men and a wonderful indication of his power to teach the people as one having authority and not as the Scribes.

To have grasped this fact, however, is not enough, even for our understanding of Matthew. In this Gospel with its pronounced systematic character, the grouping of the sayings and works of Jesus has something to do with the actual life of the communities which the Evangelist served. To clarify this connection of the Gospel of Matthew with the life of the communities let us examine for example the next to the last of Matthew's five blocks of material. This is the block concerning Jesus and his opponents, a block composed of incidents concerning Sabbath observance, concerning the charge of being in league with Beelzebub, and the incident of Jesus' relation to his mother and his brothers.

What did the Evangelist mean when he introduced this series of incidents with the inquiry made by John the Baptist from his prison? In order to understand the Evangelist's motive we must realize that in the period of Matthew there were apparently some groups who claimed that John the Baptist, not Jesus, was the Messiah. Matthew arranged his subject matter in the order indicated because the pericope provided the Christians with material which they could use in their disputations with the Baptist's followers. We can still feel the Evangelist's intention. He wanted to help the communities in some way. He wanted to advise the Christians how to bear witness for their faith against the disciples of John the Baptist.

Such considerations also dictated the compilation of the Sermon on the Mount. It contains commandments, it contains prophetic appeals, it contains sayings of wisdom, and, from the point of view of the Evangelist, Christians are to read it as an actual divine law. Matthew, by renouncing chronology in his work, was able to arrange his material in a systematic way. By so arranging his material, he made the Sermon on the Mount an ordinance governing the communities of his own age. He did not feel himself bound by the historical order of events or sayings in the life of Jesus, and for this reason he could combine saying with saying in so far as they were homogeneous.

It is probable that he also undertook some alterations in his material. We learn this from the parallel passages in the other Gospels. Perhaps, however, it is sometimes not the Evangelist who is responsible for such changes but the communities for which he is speaking. At all events there are such alterations; the best known of them is the exception which Matthew grants to the prohibition of divorce. In the case of unchastity divorce is allowed, but in the original wording of the sentence as preserved in Mark, divorce is forbidden absolutely: "What God has joined, then, man must not separate" (Mark 10:9). In trying to understand the reason for the change we may imagine a situation where a pagan wife of a Christian has a lover, and it consequently becomes impossible for the

Christian husband and for the Christian community to tolerate this situation. This, or some situation like it, may be what determined the Matthean wording of the saying and required the exception which it makes in the case of unchastity. This situation was possible only at an advanced period in the life of the Church when the Christian communities included men and women of the well-to-do classes.

We must see these and similar alterations of the sayings of Jesus in a large context. We owe them to the tendency to make possible the impossible. In their original wording some of the sayings of Jesus were not rules fitted for the common life. Later on we will see what they actually were. They seem too paradoxical to be carried out; they were impracticable. When they were connected with other sayings, which were really practicable commands, the more or less paradoxical words were transformed in the direction of a practical and living realism. In this way the paradoxical sayings became practicable and the whole mass of sayings in the Sermon on the Mount became a Christian law. The consequences of these alterations should not be underestimated. I will discuss them in the next chapters. Here I would merely emphasize in a preliminary way the fact that the programmatic character of the Sermon on the Mount depends on this unifying arrangement. The whole composition as it stands now presents an ideal of the Christian life.

The question to whom the Sermon on the Mount is addressed is in my opinion not so important for our consideration as some theologians have suggested. A careful exegesis shows that the introductory remarks at the beginning of the Sermon on the Mount present rather a picture of the general circumstances than a tradition handed down to the Evangelist. The situation as developed in Matthew contains two statements about the listeners of the sermon. Jesus is first described as seeing the crowd surrounding him and going to the top of a hill apparently not to evade the multitude, but to have a better survey. Then, when he is seated, it is his disciples who come unto him, and he teaches them. We are quite free to picture either the crowd at his feet or the disciples around him. The disciples or the crowd or both—they are the hearers of his preaching.

The uncertainty of the exegesis on this point is by no means astonishing. Matthew, we must remember, is not planning to record an historical incident, but is issuing an ordinance in discourse form. Actually, the group addressed is the Christian community the world over; it does not matter, whether disciples or crowds of Galileans are in his report the hearers of this sermon.

For a better understanding of the problem at issue we should compare Matthew's Sermon with the parallel record in Luke. Luke, it will be recalled, not only reproduces most of the elements of the Sermon on the Mount, but also provides an analogous discourse containing some of the identical material, and gives his discourse a similar setting.

His introduction runs as follows. Jesus ascends a mountain to pray, wishing to evade the crowd. He remains there during the night and "when it was day he called unto him his disciples" and with them he descends and comes in touch with the multitude and heals them all. In this situation he addresses his disciples and says: "Blessed be ye poor, for yours is the Kingdom of God." Luke may well be correct in a strict historical sense, for these beatitudes in the second person must be spoken to faithful followers; hence Luke mentions only the disciples and not the crowd. But this restriction applies only to the beatitudes. The other words of the sermon are general in their application, and the closing passage in the Lukan discourse states that the Lord has spoken in the hearing of the people as a whole. Thus, it becomes clear from this comparison that the whole question of the persons addressed is quite unimportant for the Evangelist and not decisive for interpretation.

Now we come back to the text of Matthew. As a result of our previous inquiry we may state that the Sermon on the Mount is a composite of various sayings. But the Evangelist brought these sayings and groups of sayings together in order to give a characteristic survey of Jesus' teaching. In doing so he wanted to incite the Christians of his own generation to live their lives according to these rules, and he endeavoured to present a program of Christian ethics for all generations of the Church. We could conclude this from the literary character of Matthew's Gospel and from the position of the Sermon on the Mount at the beginning of his record. Let us now consider the contents of the Sermon on the Mount from this point of view. I do not wish to interpret at this moment the several sayings as they were actually uttered by the Lord, but only the Evangelist's rendering of them.

Let us begin with the beatitudes. They are, in the opinion of Matthew, descriptions of the virtues which a Christian should exercise. They are not addressed to a general audience, but to another more specific group, and they present a doctrine about the true heirs of the Kingdom of Heaven. Who may enter into this Kingdom? Those who are poor in spirit, merciful, the peacemakers, etc. The closing sentence brings the comparison with the light, namely "let your light so shine before men, that they may see your good works and glorify your father who is in heaven," and thus reveals the identity of the group addressed. It is—in Matthew's opinion—the whole Church, the Christians who according to Paul shine as lights "in this crooked and perverse generation."

After this wonderful and impressive introduction we pass to the section which contains a commentary on some commandments of the Jewish law—comprising explanation and incrementation at the same time. Everybody knows the introductory formula: "You have heard that it was said to the men of old time . . . but I say unto you." . . . The underlying conception is that the old law has a positive value, but that the important thing for Christians is not the wording but the pure will of God. This will is not expressed with sufficient clarity in the law for men to recognize and obey it, but they must be aware of the will of God, hidden behind the wording of the commandments, and must be loyal in fulfilling it. Therefore they must take every commandment more seriously and fulfil it in a more complete way.

A few sentences prominently placed at the beginning of the entire section express the whole doctrine of a new Christian law in a few words: your righteousness shall exceed the righteousness of the Scribes and Pharisees. It may be questioned whether this small section Matthew 5:17–20 does not reflect the attitude of some Jewish-Christian communities rather than that of our Lord himself. But at any rate the closing phrase quoted above expresses very well the meaning of the commandments as given. The new righteousness, that is indeed the subject of this section of the Sermon on the Mount. The next section, Matthew 6:1–18, points to the same principle: Jesus speaks of giving alms, of prayer, of fasting in the same way, applying the standard of the new righteousness to the practices of Jewish piety. The opening clause of this section is significant. According to the older text— there is a difference between older and younger manuscripts at this point—Jesus commands that they must not do their righteousness before men to be seen of them. This is indeed the summary of the whole section.

To the next section of the Sermon on the Mount, Matthew 6:19–34, belong various groups of sayings, the commandment not to lay up treasures on earth, not to serve two masters, not to take care for life and body. Yet the section deals with but one subject. All its commandments are related to earthly goods. Thus, in the first two chapters of the Sermon on the Mount, the fifth and sixth of Matthew, after the promise of the Kingdom of God to the righteous Christian, Jesus proclaims the new law, which commands a better righteousness and forbids all entanglement in worldly affairs.

The last section of the Sermon on the Mount, the seventh chapter of Matthew's Gospel, is not so clear in its purpose as are the others. It is simply a collection of sayings, Matthew 7:1–23, which may be divided in seven paragraphs (with the exception of the two closing parables): On judging, on casting pearls before swine, the answer to prayer, the golden rule, the narrow gate, the test of goodness and the warning against self-deception. The last paragraph contains the commandment to fulfil these rules by doing them and not merely by saying "Lord, Lord!" This section is connected with the closing parables of the builders, the meaning of which is to do as the wise builder has done and not only to listen. Between the other paragraphs there is no connection at all. The problem with which we are confronted in attempting to interpret this composition may be solved by comparing the parallel passages in the Gospel of Luke.

The parallel discourse, Luke 6:20–49, begins with the beatitudes and ends with the same parables found in Matthew. Within it there appear three of the seven paragraphs given in Matthew 7:1–23, namely: the prohibition against judging, the test of goodness (about the good tree and the good fruit) and the short word, "Why do you say to me: Lord, Lord, and do not the things which I say?" These sayings have not the same wording in Luke as they have in Matthew. They are partly fuller, partly shorter than Matthew's, but there is no doubt that they treat the same subject matter in much the same manner.

The solution of the problem is quite clear. Matthew and Luke depend upon a common source; and the order of Matthew's seventh chapter is conditioned by this source. He had before him those three paragraphs and the closing parables as we may conclude from Luke. Matthew added to this material other sayings like the word about the narrow gate, in accordance with his usual practice of grouping his material in blocks. His order therefore in this seventh chapter is not a matter of content, but a matter of source. Now it is a fact that in the previous chapter Matthew also has some paragraphs common with Luke. Luke's sermon begins with the beatitudes (in a different form) and what follows is the commandment to love one's enemies, that is, the most significant part of the new law in Matthew. What underlies both texts is, no doubt, the same common source which scholars have detected in most portions of both Gospels, so far as they do not depend on Mark. What strikes us here is not the existence of this source, but the order of paragraphs common to both Gospels as well as to the supposed source. We must therefore conclude that this earlier source also contained a kind of programmatic sermon. This sermon was probably short but characteristic and apparently contained the beatitudes, the most important commandment (to love one's enemies), some different groups of sayings and the closing parables.

We see that neither Luke nor Matthew has created this type of discourse composed of single sayings and groups of sayings. There is no doubt that already in the time before our Gospels the Christian community required such a summary of their Lord's teaching. This requirement was met by our supposed source and later on by Luke and in a fuller way by Matthew.

Because it has recently become a matter of international discussion, I add here a few words concerning the name applied to this source. We call the source Q and this title is very familiar now to all who are interested in Gospel criticism the world over. The symbol Q, however, has come into common use only since the beginning of this century and it seems that today nobody remembers the precise origin of this very simple designation. Most of us suggest that it is an abbreviation of the German word "Quelle." Professor Robert Henry Lightfoot of Oxford in his Bampton Lectures *History and Interpretation of the Gospels,* following some remarks of Doctor Armitage Robinson, suggested that the symbol Q came from Doctor Robinson to Professor Julius Wellhausen of Göttingen, and that its original meaning has nothing to do with the German word but is simply a letter, the letter following P, and P according to Doctor Robinson means Peter and is the designation of the alleged source of Mark. Now Q as the next letter would designate the second source of the Synoptists, but this suggestion cannot be right, because the symbol Q is older than Wellhausen's commentaries. It appeared in Germany between 1898 and 1901 and the first book in which I find it is Professor Wernle's work *Die synoptische Frage,* published in 1899. I wrote to Professor Wernle at Basle, and he informed me that he can faintly remember the origin of the symbol Q. It was probably used for the first time in the circle of young theologians at Göttingen, including Wilhelm Bousset, Johannes Weiss and Paul Wernle himself, who required a designation without any literary or historical implications or presuppositions such as were contained in the expressions, *Apostolische Quelle, Spruch-Quelle,* Second Source etc. This is indeed the real advantage of the symbol Q, that it does not involve any presuppositions.

Indeed, we have no right to affirm anything about the literary character of the source called Q. What we may say about Q in the present context is only this, that even the source Q contained a summary of the Lord's teaching. This summary underlies the two different renditions of the Sermon on the Mount in Luke and in Matthew.

This observation is more important than one would imagine at the first glance, for, having made it, we are in a position to draw certain historical as well as theological conclusions. The first of them concerns a statement of historical fact. The first communities, let us say about 50 A.D., required a summary of the Lord's teaching in order to have rules of conduct for their own life. This gives us evidence that they believed in Jesus Christ not only as the Redeemer but also as a teacher who brought with him the new commandments of the Kingdom of Heaven.

Somebody might perhaps object that the epistles of Paul give evidence of another belief, that for Paul the Incarnation and the death of Christ were the main points of his message, that his communities looked upon Christ as Saviour and Redeemer, not as a teacher. This objection, indeed, presents a problem to us with which we will deal later.

For the moment it must be remembered that Paul in more than one passage presupposes a knowledge of sayings of Jesus within his communities, especially at Corinth. He says that the Lord has ordained that the missionaries should gain their livelihood by their preaching (I Corinthians 9:14). He does not indicate the source of this quotation, but apparently the readers are aware of its origin. In the same letter he quotes a commandment of the Lord about divorce (I Corinthians 7:10), and adds (I Corinthians 7:25) that he has no such commandment concerning virgins. We may infer that the Apostle has in his bag—or in his memory —a collection of sayings of Jesus. He reminds his readers further that he has delivered unto them the words of the Lord by which he instituted the Eucharist (I Corinthians 11:23). We must conclude, therefore, that these communities had a tradition concerning Jesus' words, perhaps also concerning his deeds.

The only question raised by Paul's teaching is, why he did not make a fuller use of this tradition in his epistles. However, for our particular task it is enough to be able to affirm that there was such a tradition in very early times. Probably there was more than one collection of sayings; at all events the existence of collections such as that contained in our alleged document Q is entirely probable, even at the time when Paul was receiving his missionary training from those who were believers before him, *i.e.*, in the thirties or at the beginning of the forties of the first century A.D.

The second conclusion to be drawn from our analysis concerns a theological matter. From the oldest known summary of Jesus' teaching we can infer what the first Christians regarded as the most characteristic features of his message. These features are clearly indicated in the agreement between Luke and Matthew in the Sermon on the Mount. First of all stands the promise of the Kingdom of God, expressed in the beatitudes. This, according to the old tradition, was the main subject of our Lord's preaching: the Kingdom of God is at hand! Next, as the common element of the section concerning the new law, comes the commandment to love one's enemy and the related prohibition against all retaliation. They were the symbol of the new attitude of men who have been won for the Gospel. Then come a few special sayings against judging and on the good trees and the good fruit, and at the end stands the exhortation to the disciples of Christ to be doers of the word and not listeners only. It is the hour of decision; only the doers will enter into the Kingdom of God! In the mind of the first Christians this was the *summary of Jesus' teaching*.

Now, a question arises from this statement. What did Jesus himself proclaim and what was the original meaning of his preaching? To answer this question we must go back from the sources created by the preachers to the subject of this preaching.

CHAPTER III

The Old Tradition About the Preaching of Jesus

WE FOUND in the previous chapter that Jesus did not teach in the form of long addresses or in a rhetorical manner. To this statement we must add the words: so far as our sources allow us to judge. Our sources are, in this case, the Gospels, with the exception of the Fourth Gospel, for the Fourth Gospel, even in its rhetorical technique, represents the mind of its author much more than the attitude of our Lord. The other Gospels are different renderings of the tradition, *i.e.*, of the stories and sayings which the Christian communities received and preserved, and from this tradition we may recognize the original forms which Jesus employed and adapted to his use. They were not the discourse in the rhetorical sense of the word, but rather the parable story, the sententious saying of the wisdom literature, the commandment and some types of prophetical appeal to the listeners, such as beatitudes, woes and exhortations.

Thus, the tradition which underlies the first three Gospels shows clearly the style and the manner of Jesus' preaching. This tradition about the words and deeds of Jesus is the only authentic source of our knowledge about Jesus' earthly days, not the framework created for it by the Evangelists, as they strove to combine isolated incidents and to give a consecutive account of the whole of Jesus' career. Any one seeking reliable evidence about this career must go back from the Gospels to the tradition because the so-called Synoptic Gospels are not literary works written by literary authors, but compositions of various elements of the tradition arranged in a different order and enclosed in a different framework. German Gospel criticism is now at a stage where we take this difference between the original tradition and the work of the Evangelists very seriously.

The method of the Gospel criticism, called *Formgeschichte* or Form-criticism, asks in the first place, what the tradition was and meant, and not what the author of the Gospel thought, desired and described. *Formgeschichte* suggests that the old tradition contained only small units of material (short stories, parables, sayings and groups of sayings) and almost no biographical framework. This conclusion follows from the character of the oldest of our Gospels, the Gospel of Mark. Every reader interested in these literary questions can readily ascertain for himself that the major portion of this Gospel is composed of small pericopes or series of pericopes, of brief accounts or individual incidents, of some few sayings and a very few parables. The only address of any length found in Mark, the discourse on the last things, Mark 13, is again composed of individual sayings or groups of sayings. The Evangelist himself has created the framework by which all these units of material are held together; thus in Mark 3:6 he indicates that the incidents reported in Mark 2 and 3:1–5 were the cause of the Pharisaic antagonism against our Lord. Or he informs us that Jesus often spoke in parables after having given some examples of this type of subject matter in chapter 4. In reality the Gospel of Mark is a mosaic, and its character as a mosaic shows that when Mark wrote his book he was in possession of a tradition comprising merely separate narratives and sayings.

Another indication of the nature of the early tradition about Jesus comes from the speeches in Acts, which, authentic or not, present at least the manner in which the first Christians preached. Analyzed as to their structure, these sermons reveal that the early Christian preacher in his preaching usually made brief mention of Jesus' earthly life, his miracles, his crucifixion and his resurrection. This holds good for all missionary sermons in Acts with the exception only of Paul's address at Athens with its well-known special character. But all other missionary speeches in Acts, in chapters 2, 3, 5, 10 and 13, contain a short summary of Jesus' career, his deeds and his death. Of course, the preacher found it necessary to illustrate these summaries of the main facts of Jesus' life and for this purpose he needed short narratives of individual incidents and not a single long biography, for the latter would have been too long for his sermon. This, then, seems to be the origin and the earliest stage of the tradition concerning the events of the life of Jesus.

We turn now to the tradition concerning the sayings. It seems highly probable that they originated in a similar way. The Christians needed rules to govern their lives before the end of the world, rules not only for individual conduct, but also for the social life within the communities. For this reason they collected the sayings and parables of Jesus, adapting them where necessary to their own circumstances. We have already seen how Paul intimates in the first letter to the Corinthians that he possesses a collection of this type. He makes use of it in order to solve some community problems such as marriage and divorce or the support of the missionaries.

The preservation of the words of Jesus motivated in this way was accomplished in a twofold manner. Some sayings were handed down in connection with an event of Jesus' life. The incident brought out the meaning of the saying. An illustration of this is the answer which Jesus gave to the man who wanted to bury his father before becoming a disciple. Jesus said to him: "Let the dead bury their dead." Here a word of Jesus is preserved in connection with an account of an event for the simple reason that the word would not be impressive without some indication of the circumstances under which it was spoken, in this case the would-be-disciple's own request. This holds good also for longer stories, for example, the healing of the paralytic. The reader can understand the meaning of Jesus' words only by grasping the whole situation.

Before we turn to the second manner of preserving

the sayings of our Lord, it must be emphasized how cautiously the tradition treated the words of Jesus preserved within such incidents, while often feeling perfectly free to alter the remaining text of the story. For example, the story of the centurion's servant is preserved in a longer form by Luke and in a shorter one by Matthew, but the words which Jesus spoke to the centurion are quite the same in both Gospels (Matthew combines another saying, 8:11, 12, with this incident, but it does not belong to the story). Also the preceding request of the centurion which actually is expressed in Luke by friends, in Matthew by the centurion himself, has the same wording in both Gospels. Another example of this reliability is presented by the so-called unknown Gospel recently discovered in Egypt and now preserved in the British Museum. It contains the story of the healing of the leper in a form which differs extensively from the Synoptists. But the wording of the sick man's request and of Jesus' answer is the same as that found in the canonical Gospels. This furnishes a good illustration of the conservative tendency of the tradition which preserved the words of our Lord even when the framework was altered.

Besides this manner of collecting the sayings of Jesus within a story there was another manner. Many words of Jesus were handed down without a story framework because the record of the incident was unnecessary. The sayings were intelligible in themselves. Either the tradition has lost sight of the occasion at

which they were spoken or Jesus spoke these words
without any special occasion as a teacher, expressing
his idea in a striking watchword.

Of course we cannot recognize whether there was
any special occasion or not. At any rate these sayings
were handed down isolated, without the framework
of a story. This is the case with the sayings which were
combined in order to form the Sermon on the Mount.
In some instances this manner of handing down tradition creates difficulties for us. The original meaning
of a saying is sometimes lost because the framework
of its setting is missing. A case in point is the saying
Matthew 7:6, "Give not that which is holy unto
the dogs and cast not your pearls before swine"—
a parable, the original application of which we do
not know. But there are very few sayings in the
Gospels the meaning of which is so obscured. More
frequently we must suggest another difficulty. Sometimes apparently the tradition has inserted some
other sayings in the place of a lost meaning or has set
the original word in a context which gives an interpretation not in accordance with the original meaning.
This may be the case with the saying about the eye as
the light of the body, Matthew 6:22. Here the context, the saying on treasures, clearly applies the parable to the heart of man—and it may be questioned
whether this was the original meaning. Some examples
of insertions we shall find later in the prohibition
against anxieties and in the beatitudes.

In considering the different forms in which the

tradition has preserved the sayings of Jesus we get an impression of the manner of teaching which our Lord used during his lifetime. It was not the way of an eloquent preacher who influences the people by his brilliant technique of speaking. It was rather the way of an adviser and a teacher who visits men in their homes in order to help, to give counsel, to criticize and to proclaim. But he does not come as a teacher in his own right, he speaks as an ambassador; indeed it may truly be said that on the whole the Fourth Gospel is right in emphasizing this point of view: "My teaching is not mine but his that sends me."

It seems to be necessary in this connection to emphasize the great difference between the manner of Jesus' teaching and the manner of the great philosophers of Greece. The so-called Socratic method teaches by dialogue. Socrates tried to draw out from the mind of his pupils the thoughts necessary for the discussion; every partner of the discussion has the duty of collaborating in a philosophical sense. Jesus— if the tradition of the Synoptists is reliable—did not discuss any subject in such a way. He proclaimed something, he demanded something, he promised something, but without any human intermediation. The discussions with Pharisees and Scribes reported in Mark 2, 3, 7, 10, 12 have their own character. In these sections the opponents put their questions only in order to tempt him, to embarrass him, to harm him. None of the replies of the opponents have any actual value for the story; they only give Jesus occasions to decide a case or to warn his enemies. None of his opponents can further the discussion by putting stimulating questions.

In the later stage of Greek philosophy, during the Hellenistic age, philosophers did not discuss their problems with disciples but spoke rather in the streets in the presence of the general public. Of course these hearers were not able to collaborate in any way. Therefore the questions intended to promote discussion had now to be put by the teachers themselves. They did it in the manner familiar to us from the epistles of Paul and James, by introducing the questions with the formula: "perhaps somebody would object" or something like this. This method also was not suited to Jesus' needs, because it was not his task to develop and prove ideas as men do in their discussions and deliberations. For him all human questions and incidents were only occasions to preach the Gospel of the coming Kingdom. In comparing the methods of the Greek philosophers with those of Jesus we can understand the difference between a proclamation in the name of God and the development of human ideas.

The comparison of Jesus' methods of teaching with the manner used by the Prophets and Rabbis is more helpful for our understanding of the Gospels. Jesus uses the well-known forms of the prophetical address such as blessings and woes; Luke presents woes in his text of the Sermon on the Mount immediately after the beatitudes. But one difference between Jesus and the Prophets must be emphasized; he does not report personal experiences of ecstatic nature like the Prophets; he does not speak about his intercourse with his Heavenly Father. The one word Luke 10:18, "I saw Satan fallen as lightning from heaven," does not contradict this statement because it is meant as an apocalyptic prophecy: the end of the reign of Satan will come. Thus the background of this saying is an apocalyptic conviction, not a personal experience which came in a dream or in a moment of ecstasy. We find no notice in the Gospels that Jesus in an historic moment of his life was taken away from his profession by a divine commandment like Amos. Therefore we must conclude that he did not tell anything about such experiences.

The only incident one might cite to the contrary is that of Jesus' Baptism. The story implies that Jesus heard in the Baptist's preaching the voice of God announcing the coming of the Kingdom, a fact which the Evangelical express in terms of the voice from heaven. But Jesus never mentioned this experience in his sayings, nor did he ever allude to apparitions of heavenly beings as many of the prophets had done. The Transfiguration is an apparent rather than an actual exception to this rule, for it tells of a revelation given to the disciples, not to their master. Jesus, it seems, does not require the mediation of heavenly beings to understand the Father's will. His knowledge of God and his consciousness of His will are direct, continuous and uninterrupted.

There is another difference between Jesus and the Scribes. The Scribe is obliged to give evidence for his opinion from the Scriptures; he has no authority himself. Jesus, as it is said in the Gospel, speaks as "one having authority and not as the Scribes." Sometimes he takes arguments from the Scriptures, but he does not need to quote from the Old Testament again and again, for he proclaims the will of God in virtue of his own consciousness of God. This is the reason why the Scribes cannot bear his teaching. It is a great heresy for the Jews to teach about God and divine revelation without any exegetical evidence. However, there is a similarity between the form of Jesus' teaching and that of the Scribes. This is to be found particularly in Jesus' use of sententious sayings, of commandments and of parables.

Lastly we may look at the great master of Buddhism and compare Jesus' method of teaching with his. There are, no doubt, some similarities. Both call disciples to assist them; both utter their message by word of mouth only, not in writing. Nevertheless there is a great difference which a brief glance at both traditions will reveal to us. Buddha speaks mostly in connected discourses the form of which is fitted to be retained in memory. There is a natural connection between the phrases, there is a scheme of introductory remarks: *e.g.*, he says in the Sermon of Benares: "This, ye ascetics, is the noble truth about suffering: birth is suffering, old age is suffering, illness is suffering," etc. "This, ye ascetics, is the noble truth about the origin of suffering," etc. Thirdly: "This, ye ascetics, is the noble truth about the oppression of suffering," etc. Or, in the speech concerning the truth about suffering, he says: "And what, ye monks, is birth?" Some answers follow, namely: "to be born, to enter in a womb," etc. The closing phrase runs: "This, ye monks, is what we call birth. . . . And what, ye monks, is death? To fade, to pass away. . . . This, ye monks, is what we call death."

In the teaching of Jesus the only comparable elements are the stereotyped phrases with which certain of the parables begin, and the introductory formula used in one portion of the Sermon on the Mount: "You have heard that it was said to them of old . . . but I say unto you . . ." The recurrence of this formula, however, is to be attributed to the editorial activity of the Evangelist rather than to the frequency of its use by Jesus. We therefore look in vain for extensive similarities between the form of Jesus' teaching and the form of Buddha's instruction.

The reason lies deeper. Buddha wants to save men by knowledge, Jesus by proclaiming the will of God. The one demands insight, the other repentance and obedience. Insight leads to resignation from the world; the consequence of the Christian obedience is that Christians may stand in the midst of the world and render service to God by working and collaborating within the world. Therefore, Buddha can teach by an appeal to human reason and in forms fitted to common understanding, in order to prove that the worldly

existence has no hope. Jesus must proclaim supernatural demands and promises and speaks, therefore,
like a prophet; in doing so he gives evidence of the
divine will and demands obedience in the name of
God.

This survey of other prophecies and teachings
seemed necessary to me for a better understanding of
Jesus' method of instruction. We now have an impression of the way in which Jesus preached and
taught. We see him passing from one man to another
answering their questions, solving their problems,
healing their illnesses. This is the content of the
stories in the Gospels. We also hear Jesus proclaiming before the people and the disciples the coming
Kingdom of Heaven and the commandments of his
Heavenly Father; we hear him teaching by means of
sententious sayings of the type familiar to us from the
wisdom literature and illustrating his teachings by
metaphors and parables.

It is important for the understanding of our Lord's
message that we should be aware of this method.
Form-criticism ventures to go back to those small
units of which Jesus' teaching consists, to detach them
from their framework and to study their original
meaning. Such units of tradition are the elements of
which the Sermon on the Mount is composed. It is a
summary of characteristic sayings whose historical occasion we do not know. They were brought together by
the early tradition within the communities in order to
form a kind of Christian law. Since this was their

purpose the Evangelists added other sayings of our
Lord to the collection which existed in the days of Q,
thus completing or explaining the older tradition.

It seems possible, of course, that at this occasion
some non-authentic elements were included in the
record by the Evangelists, partly because they were
already connected with the original sayings, partly
because they were suited to illustrate or explain the
authentic words. I am speaking here of possibilities
only. Insertions can frequently be identified as such,
by the way in which they disturb the connection between sayings, and by a comparison of Matthew and
Luke. But we are not always in a position to decide
whether these insertions are genuine words of Jesus
or not. At any rate, I am not convinced that the meaning of Jesus' words, especially in the Sermon on the
Mount, was seriously falsified by such insertions, and
the general impression made by our investigation of
the tradition is a favourable one. Such investigations
are necessary not only for the more or less hypothetical
reconstruction of the original wording of the sayings,
but also for an examination of their original meaning.
To this we must now turn.

CHAPTER IV

The Sayings of Jesus

WE HAVE gained an impression of the nature of the Gospel Tradition as well as of the method of Jesus' teaching. Now we turn to the question which lies at the heart of scientific exegesis and ask what the original meaning of Jesus' sayings really was. We shall concern ourselves first of all with a group of sayings which are handed down in Matthew as well as in Luke; by Luke not in his text of the Sermon on the Mount, but in the twelfth chapter of his Gospel. This group of sayings consists of the warning against cares of this world. (Matt. 6:25–34.) "Be not anxious for your life, what ye shall eat or what ye shall drink, nor yet for your body, what ye shall put on." This is a typical block of material, for we find in it a number of characteristic formal differences between Matthew and Luke; it is typical too, because in dealing with these sayings we find ourselves confronted with the greatest of all the problems of the Sermon on the Mount: are these rules and counsels practicable, and if so, is their fulfilment desirable? In other words, is the Sermon on the Mount a law, a message, a vision or a fancy?

About the differences between Matthew and Luke a few words will suffice. Some of the expressions are typical of Matthew and of the Christian communities

44

for which he wrote; we know them from other passages. Matthew likes to call God the Heavenly Father. He likes the term "righteousness" used in a nomistic Jewish sense; remember his account of Jesus' baptism and the answer of Jesus: "thus it becomes us to fulfil all righteousness." Hence, in this group of sayings Matthew speaks of God's Kingdom and His righteousness, while Luke speaks only of the Kingdom of God. Matthew, probably in accordance with the religious language of his communities, prefers the more liturgical expressions like the "birds of the air"; Luke uses a more realistic form of phrase and has Jesus speak of the "ravens."

In all these cases it is probable that Matthew did not follow the tradition handed down to him; instead he used the terminology familiar to him and to his communities, a terminology of a more Jewish character. In these cases, then, Luke probably has the authentic wording, a wording without signs of a special literary or technical terminology. But there are other instances where the opposite is true. In some passages Luke writes in his own, more Hellenistic, more literary style. He turns the rhetorical questions, which Jesus employed after the fashion familiar in Jewish usage, into dogmatic assertions. He writes "the life is more than meat" instead of the more popular and more Jewish form "is not the life more than meat?" Luke also uses literary constructions in preference to popular ones. He likes words of a higher type. In the section on cares, with which we are dealing, the

best example is the word *meteorizein*—*i.e.*, be anxious
or worried—which occurs in no other biblical passage.
In all these instances Matthew preserves the original
wording.

In turning now to investigate the meaning of the
section under discussion, we must begin with two observations formulated in accordance with the method
of *Formgeschichte*.

(1) The word in Matthew 6:34, "Be not anxious
for the morrow, for the morrow will take care for itself. Sufficient unto the day is the evil thereof" was
originally a separate saying and does not properly belong to this context. It is not found in Luke and is
scarcely of the right character to serve as the closing
sentence of this important section. It has its parallels
in Rabbinic writings (*cf.* in the Bab. Talmud, Sota
48 b, Sanhedrin 100 b) and its inherent character is
actually that of a common popular maxim. As such it
is obviously out of place after the heroic command of
the preceding verse: "Seek ye first His Kingdom."
This last is apparently the authentic ending of the section, and the word in 6:34 is an insertion of the kind
I described above (p. 43).—It may be a maxim once
used by Jesus or a non-authentic saying quoted here
as a commentary on the words of our Lord.

(2) My second statement is this. The verse, Matthew 6:27, "Who can by anxious care add one cubit
unto his height?" is difficult to explain and should
also be regarded in all probability as an independent
saying, inserted here and connected with the whole

section by the addition of the words "by anxious care."
If we omit these words, the saying has a clear meaning: ye have no power over the smallest things; God
is the Lord and He alone. Because this is the most
probable interpretation, the saying is out of harmony
with the context and should be omitted from our section, though without prejudice to its ultimate authenticity.

The whole section as it now stands before us com-
prises a twofold warning. "Be not anxious for food,
be not anxious for clothing. Look at the ravens, how
they live, consider the lilies, how they grow—they are
not anxious, God provides for them. Do not care for
such things, but only for God's Kingdom, and all
these things shall be added unto you!"

In the face of these warnings we are obliged to ask:
what did Jesus command, what did he prohibit? Did
he mean that the disciples should live without cares
and provision for the future? Did he really mean to
recommend imprudence? Or are his words to be interpreted as a serious and therefore purposely exag-
gerated warning against the greed for gain? Exegesis
has long tried to answer these questions. The most
important explanations are the following.

(1) The exhortation against cares is to be taken
literally as an absolute prohibition and represents a
radical but practicable law: you must actually live
without cares. For better understanding the explanation is sometimes offered that in the circumstances under which Jesus lived it was easier to fulfil this com-

mandment than it would be today. In the ancient East man could live with little. At any rate, the rule is to be taken literally and must be fulfilled. To be true to their Faith Christians ought, according to this interpretation, actually to live without cares.

(2) The word is not to be taken too literally. Jesus means that we should not overemphasize the importance of purely worldly occupations. Only the form is that of an absolute prohibition, and the purpose is to encourage a serious religious attitude which is directed only toward the Kingdom of Heaven. In this pursuit the followers of Jesus should not be embarrassed by worldly anxieties.

(3) The word is to be taken literally, but the warning holds good only for the disciples: they are and ought to be released from cares, *i.e.*, from the need of earning their living, for the communities should support them. This theory, which takes the Sermon on the Mount as an address to the disciples only, is wrong on the face of it, because it depends upon the setting into which the Sermon on the Mount has been placed—and this is the work of the Evangelist, as we have already stated (*cf*. pp. 42–43). Here we see how dangerous it is to assume that the Sermon on the Mount was spoken to a specific group. No, the section must be interpreted without regard to the question of who is addressed. Hence, we can afford to ignore this explanation in our further consideration of the passage.

(4) The word is to be taken eschatologically, the

commandment applying only to the interim between Jesus' day and the end of the world. This is the interpretation suggested by the well-known theory that Jesus' ethic is an "interim ethic." The interpretation has this in its favour that, for the duration of the brief interim, man can actually exist without making the forbidden provisions. But the theory effectively limits the validity of Jesus' commandments, and is thus beset with difficulties.

(5) The word is to be taken eschatologically, but in a sense other than that assigned to it in No. 4. The commandment proclaims the law of the Kingdom, the pure will of God, without any limitation by or accommodation to the conditions of this world. The word is to be interpreted literally as an absolute prohibition just because it is not confined in its application to a period, but is valid for eternity.

What, then, shall we say concerning these different interpretations? What position shall we take in the matter? I think that our first duty must be to give an interpretation that is historically defensible, *i.e.*, to answer in a trustworthy manner the simple question: what did Jesus mean when he spoke in this way? Some general observations should help us in arriving at a valid conclusion.

First of all we should look at the closing phrase of the entire section, the phrase: "Seek the Kingdom of God and all these things shall be added unto you!" It is quite clear that this is not an oracle applying to this world; it would be quite out of harmony with the spirit of the Gospel to have Jesus promise such worldly things to those who accept the Gospel for their life here and now. Apparently the meaning of the sentence is: you must seek the Kingdom of God and nothing else! And when the Kingdom comes then all your needs will be fulfilled! Consequently it is the underlying assumption of the whole pericope that the hearers will live to see the end of the world. They are not obliged to provide for their livelihood in a distant future, for there will be no distant future at all. Because by this saying the eyes of Jesus' hearers are directed toward the coming Kingdom, we are right in characterizing the whole saying as an eschatological one.

Once this has become clear, we may proceed to add a second observation. The motivation of the command to improvidence on the part of the faithful seems at first sight to be a purely rational one: do just as the ravens do; live like the lilies! It is possible to live without cares; therefore do so! But this conclusion would be wrong; actually Jesus does not refer to a more natural form of conduct, illustrated by ravens and lilies, but to God who has created the ravens as well as the lilies and has in this way revealed His original purpose for His creatures. The purpose of the Creator was indeed to establish a form of existence which would be free from all cares and worldly anxieties. Jesus does not say only "when the Kingdom comes you will be freed from cares"—and therefore he does not grant that till the crisis man must live in anxiety. Rather, Jesus says in the name of God: "you men who want to be citizens of God's Kingdom before its actual coming, you must fulfil the pure will of God even now and live a life without wordly anxieties, for this is God's will and purpose." He does not speak, then, as a prophet of human happiness, but as a prophet of the *divine will*. For this reason he does not consider all worldly questions which would occur to us in this connection—neither the duties of a father of a large family nor the obligations of statesmanship, of industry and trade. The pure will of God does not suffer any restriction.

Now we are in a position to decide between the five interpretations of our pericope previously listed. Jesus proclaims in an absolute way the pure will of God. This will is not confined to an interim and is thus not valid only for the period till the end of the world; it is God's actual demand upon men at all times and for all time. But it will attain its full validity only in the Kingdom of God. It is the sign of this passing age that the fulfillment of God's will is hampered and embarrassed by the conditions of our worldly existence. In the face of the coming end Jesus proclaims God's demand without regard to any such considerations. God's will does not depend upon the eschatological hope and expectation; it is eternal, like God. The eschatological expectation, however, gives the occasion for the proclamation of the divine will, without regard to the circumstances of everyday existence. The eschatalogical expectation makes men free from all conditions of this world, free to understand what is the pure, unconditional will of God. Therefore of the various interpretations of our passage given above, the last seems to be correct; the passage is to be taken *in an absolute sense because it is eschatological*. The question whether the prohibition so interpreted is important for the world of today does not concern us in the present context. I will discuss it in the last chapter. For the moment we content ourselves with the solution we have found.

Our contention then is that the warning against anxieties is the expression of a religious radicalism, not a rigid radicalism, but an eschatological one. Let us apply this solution also to the other absolute commands and prohibitions, and turn now to the best known of all passages of the Sermon on the Mount, the sayings about retaliation and about love of one's enemies. Everybody knows the commandment: "Whoever smites thee on the right cheek, turn to him the other also" and "Love your enemies." Clearly the paradoxical character of these words is still greater than that of the words in the section about anxiety. For all that Jesus forbids in these passages is the natural psychological reaction against injustice, enmity and hatred.

Let us look for a moment at the form which the tradition takes in the two Gospels, Matthew and Luke. Both present the passages in question in the same context, *i.e.*, in the nucleus of the Sermon on the Mount taken over by the Evangelist from the source

Q. In presenting these sayings Matthew uses the formula which serves as a framework for a number of other sayings: "You have heard that it has been said . . . but I say unto you." Luke presents the sayings without this formula; hence cautious interpreters will not take this scheme as a basis for their interpretation. Also, Luke has apparently altered the sequence of the sayings; he has inserted the sentences on retaliation in the middle of the section about the love of enemies. In consequence, he was compelled to repeat the commandment of love before the concluding reference to God *who is kind unto the unthankful and to the evil*. This repetition destroys the whole form of the saying and is apparently wrong. Furthermore, Luke has inserted the so-called Golden Rule in this context, *i.e.*, the commandment that you must do unto men as you wish men to do unto you. The Golden Rule we shall need to regard as a separate saying. Formal as well as exegetical considerations combine to urge this conclusion, for the Golden Rule is a maxim of the type familiar to us from the wisdom literature and has parallels within this realm in more than one country. This Golden Rule with its philosophy of "measure for measure" is quite out of harmony with the heroic sentiments of our sayings.

We shall therefore do well to follow the wording of Matthew in dealing with the sayings about retaliation and love of enemy, making due allowances for the introductory formula which may be a Matthean addition, and for the exhortation to give to every one who asks and not to turn away from him who would borrow, which may originally have been separate sayings. Finally, it is difficult to decide between the two forms of the closing phrase of this section: "Be perfect as your Father is perfect" in Matthew and "be merciful as your Father is merciful" in Luke. Perhaps the latter form is meant as a transition to the following sentence in Luke, "judge not." Probably the word "perfect" in Matthew is meant to characterize an attitude which is better than the attitude of the publicans mentioned before. If this is true, the form of the saying preserved in Matthew is original and expresses a very simple meaning, as is usual in such closing phrases. Jesus is not concerned with the philosophical question whether or not a man can actually be perfect.

Thus, we have before us two groups of commands: (1) love your enemies and pray for your persecutors (this is the text of the oldest manuscripts in Matthew) —(2) a group of three commandments: whoever smites thee on the right cheek, turn to him the other also; if anybody take thy coat by a lawsuit, let him have thy cloak also; and whoever forces thee to accompany him as a guard one mile,—this compulsion is a kind of official demand—go with him two!

What is the meaning of all these commands? We start with the great command to love one's enemies. We must not seek to escape from the full weight of the problem by supposing that, when Jesus here speaks of an enemy, he means first and foremost the national enemy. This interpretation is improbable, because the national enemy would need to be the Roman, and we would thus find Jesus meddling in a political problem which, as we know from another passage, from his word about paying tribute to Cæsar, he wanted to leave unsolved. Moreover, it may well be questioned, whether the ancient Orient had a conception of nationality, such as could produce the idea of a national enemy.

No, in this word about loving one's enemy Jesus is apparently thinking of private enemies—enemies who hail one before a judge, bad neighbours, etc. This is the real meaning of the word enemy for his listeners. So understood the command is much more difficult to fulfil than if we give it a limited political sense. It is the private enemy whom the simple farmer or workman really hates with all the fervour of his heart. Hatred of a national enemy is less intense and harder to develop. Hatred of the enemy is not familiar in the trenches; the real national hate is the work of the stay-at-homes, not of soldiers. The most common and intense hatred is that directed against one's private enemy, *e.g.*, the unfriendly neighbour, the competitor in labour, the malicious superior or ruler. And this hatred Jesus forbids, *i.e.*, he forbids a natural psychological reaction against injustice and hostile deeds. He forbids it because hatred is opposed to the will of God.

The other group of sayings, the sayings against retaliation, gives the same impression. Here various acts of injustice are mentioned: the blow on the cheek, the lawsuit, of course without reasonable arguments, the compulsion to some required acts. Here the command is again most radical. The command is not to "suffer these things," but to "give or do more than they require of you." Jesus not only forbids any hostile reaction, but demands actions of love toward the enemy. His commandment is opposed to all the natural feeling of the human heart—if we are really honest and confess what our natural inclinations are under such circumstances.

We are now in a position to give our interpretation of these two commands so strangely contrary to all those reactions which men view as legitimately human. We may grant that the form of the command, especially in the sayings on retaliation, is hyperbolic, in the Oriental manner. The type of overt act to which Jesus alludes by way of illustration shows it clearly. But the word really holds good not only for the case in question but for all expressions of hatred. Hence this formal observation must not be permitted to weaken in any way the seriousness of the command given. What Jesus proclaims here is again the pure will of God; and God demands that man should forego retaliation and hatred completely, He demands that man should be friendly and well disposed even to his most violent and vehement antagonists. It is not a matter of legal defence, of legitimate anger, of resistance against power unjustly applied.

Jesus disregards all these possibilities, for they are determined by circumstances and perhaps by necessities of life in this world,—but this world will come to an end. Thus we see again and again: What we have before us are radical commands, an expression of the pure will of God, in no way weakened by the consideration of human necessities. This radicalism is an eschatological one. *Because* Jesus considers the Kingdom of God alone, he finds it possible to leave all worldly affairs, all human requirements, all the circumstances of the human life out of consideration.

This interpretation holds good also for the other radical commands of the Sermon on the Mount. They express an absolute demand for the renunciation of all things which might separate man from God and His Kingdom.

These radical sayings are often expressed in an hyperbolic manner, hyperbole belonging to the style of Oriental sayings. But we are not allowed to mitigate the severity of the commandments by realizing this fact. Furthermore, these sayings start sometimes from a particular incident of human life. We are obliged to apply the radical words of Jesus to all similar cases, for while he gives a commandment in terms of one incident, he means by these commandments to proclaim the true will of God generally.

An instance of this type is first of all the command to pluck out any member that causes one to stumble, for it is better that the eye or hand should perish than that the whole body should be cast into hell. In the Sermon on the Mount this word is connected with the warning against adultery which deepens the commandment of the Old Testament in an impressive way. Jesus says that adultery begins with the lustful look. He continues appropriately with our saying: "If your right eye cause you to sin, pluck it out and cast it away!" But in Mark 9:43 and Matthew 18:8 we read the same word as an isolated saying which begins with the hand and the foot rather than with the eye. This indicates that the connection with the warning against adultery cannot be taken as original, for the word refers not to any one specific member of the body and its loss but to every kind of sacrifice which may be necessary for a disciple of Jesus. If anything prevents entrance into the coming Kingdom, those who want to become citizens of this Kingdom must renounce it.

A second example of this type is the prohibition against anger and invective which forms the interpretation of the sixth commandment. Manslaughter begins with anger and insult—that is the meaning of this interpretation. Indeed, such feelings and words of anger are a natural reaction in some moments of our life, but Jesus forbids them because they are contrary to the divine will. He proclaims here not only an enlargement of the old Jewish law, but a new attitude of man.

We interpret the prohibition against judging (Matt. 7:1) and the exhortation not to lay up treasures (Matt. 6:19) in the same way. Jesus refers here to practices in human life that are common and sometimes quite legitimate, but from the point of view of the coming Kingdom they are forbidden. They are significant for the condition of the old world; in a new world they will be superfluous, and the followers of Jesus must be representatives of this new world within the old age. Finally we may remember the words against oaths and divorce. Again and again we discover to our sorrow that the word of men is not reliable and that not every marriage is a true marriage "for better—for worse, for richer—for poorer, in sickness and in health." Divorce provides a possibility of escape from this false kind of marriage. Oaths protect men from unreliable assurances. Therefore, oaths and divorce seem necessary to us as sinful men, but they are dependent upon the imperfect conditions under which we live and therefore must be abandoned even now by those who would fulfil the absolute will of God.

In conclusion, let us summarize the testimony provided by all these commands. The command to love one's enemies Jesus motivates by an argument which seems, at first sight, purely rational: the sun rises on the wicked men and on the good, the rain falls on the just and on the unjust. Here impartiality in the natural order is apparently taken as a criterion of Christian conduct. But this appearance is wrong, for Jesus does not refer to natural processes but to God the Creator who gives the same gift to the good as well as to the wicked. It is the paradoxical kindness of God to which Jesus refers, not the order of nature; and God's own paradox is the basis of Jesus' own paradoxical demand. For this reason Jesus' demand is the true expression of the divine will.

In the same way the prohibition of oaths refers to God Himself. Man cannot swear without interfering with the rights of God, for in swearing he disposes of God as the witness of his oath. The prohibition of divorce is expressed in Mark 10:9 (but not in the Sermon on the Mount) with an explicit reference to God: "What God has joined together, let not man put asunder." Thus, in the view of Jesus, divorce also is a destruction of God's work and therefore an interference with His rights. We may find a similar attitude towards the law expressed in the warning against anger and invective, because in this commandment is involved an enlargement and deepening of the Jewish law: Jesus emphasizes that only such an enlargement does justice to the original divine will revealed in the commandments. God's will demands more than the wording of the law expresses and this is recognizable now, in the last hour, in face of the coming Kingdom. Therefore the prohibition against cares as well as the command to pluck out any member that causes one to stumble (in its Marcan form) refers expressly to the Kingdom of God or to "Life," *i.e.*, the Kingdom of Heaven. God wills to enter into human life; therefore man must acknowledge His sovereign will: "Seek ye first His Kingdom!"

True, an explicit reference to the eschatological expectation is missing in some groups of sayings; in the prohibition of anger and invective, of oaths and of divorce (mark the difference between Jesus' words and the admonitions of Paul (I Cor. 7), which are expressly conditioned by an eschatological outlook). Some critics might therefore question the eschatological background of these sayings in general, but it seems to me that such a criticism would be wrong for two reasons.

(1) It is legitimate to suppose that the whole message of our Lord has an eschatological background. The summary of his preaching according to the Synoptic Gospels is the prophetic call to repentance: "Repent, for the Kingdom of Heaven is at hand." Most of his parables as well as his own interpretation of his healings point to the coming Kingdom.

(2) The Sermon on the Mount in its introduction bears witness to its eschatological orientation. The beatitudes promise the Kingdom of Heaven to the disinherited and hopeless men of this world.

In this connection we are to consider the problem of the beatitudes. As everybody knows, in Matthew there are more beatitudes than in Luke, and the Matthean blessings are expressed in the third person while the shorter text, in Luke, addresses men in the second person. The reason for this difference becomes apparent when we investigate the content of the blessings in both Gospels. The Lukan text addresses one group of men: the disinherited. Jesus proclaims that these men, his hearers, will be the true heirs of the Kingdom of God. Though he blesses the poor, those who hunger, those who weep and those who are hated, it is really one and the same group that he has in mind throughout and that he characterizes in terms of the various aspects of its unfortunate plight. The Kingdom of God will bring a reversal of all worldly positions, and those who are repudiated and expelled now will "enter in." This is the burden of all apocalyptic prophecy and the meaning also of the Lukan beatitudes.

In the Matthean text we find additional beatitudes: the blessings of the meek and of the merciful and of the pure in heart and of the peacemakers. These blessings concern not one and the same group of people, but different groups of virtuous men. Jesus mentions them, he does not address them, for this form of the beatitudes uses the third person. This formal difference is paralleled by a somewhat fuller description. Matthew describes those who are blessed at greater length. Such an enlargement seems necessary in order to avoid mistakes. The men who are addressed in Luke are blessed because they are the humble and devout hearers of Jesus. In Matthew the men are referred to in the third person; it does not matter whether they are present or not. At any rate, their virtues are described in such a way that everybody can recognize them. Not the poor are praised, but the poor in spirit, not the hungry, but those who hunger after righteousness.

We are now in a position to discuss the question of authenticity. It seems to me that the beatitudes in Luke form a real address to Jesus' hearers, in Matthew a catalogue of qualities which are required in Christian communities. Thus, the text of Luke seems to be the original wording. Matthew apparently wanted to give a description of the virtues which Christians should exercise, and therefore he added some other sayings which perhaps are authentic too, but do not belong to the original group of beatitudes. If this is right we may say that the Lukan group of beatitudes has an eschatological meaning. It is a prophecy concerning the Kingdom of God. This coming Kingdom is promised to the humble and disinherited hearers of Jesus; in this age weeping and suffering, in the coming world gladness and glory. Jesus adapted to his own hearers the old hope expressed in the Psalms: "They that sow in tears shall reap in joy," *i.e.*, he promises the Kingdom of Heaven to them.

This eschatological background lies behind all deeds and words of Jesus. This does not mean that all of Jesus' promises and prophecies are promises and prophecies of the coming world. Some of them are, but others are not. However, the reason why the words were spoken and why the deeds were done, is the coming of the new world. The sayings of the Sermon on the Mount were uttered by Jesus in order to prepare men for the Kingdom. It was his purpose in these sayings to proclaim the will of God in all its severity, the absolute divine will, unconditioned by the circumstances of this world order. This will is of course the law of the Kingdom of God, but under the conditions provided by our earthly life this will in its paradox is a stumbling block for men. We should not mitigate or weaken this fact. We must rather emphasize the paradoxical radicalism of the commands proclaimed by Jesus in the face of the coming Kingdom. When we have recognized this radicalism, our next question must be: what is the relation of this eschatological radicalism to Jewish legalism?

CHAPTER V

The Jewish Law and the Law of the Kingdom

THE Sermon on the Mount, on the whole, is a collection of radical, absolute commands and sayings. They are radical and absolute because the man who uttered them did not consider the circumstances of our life and the conditions of this world. He looks only to the coming world, the Kingdom of Heaven. We stated that the eschatological background is presupposed also in passages which would appear, when isolated, to be no more than proverbial sayings or maxims. But they were proclaimed because the Kingdom of God was at hand, and the eschatological reference transposes them to a higher level. They have a greater validity because they have been incorporated in the law of the coming Kingdom. They no longer give expression to human wisdom as they would if regarded in isolation as proverbial sayings, but they present God's demand in the time of crisis.

The two closing parables of the builders, *e.g.*, could express, if they were isolated, the warning of every Jewish teacher to his hearers: you must act and not only listen! But we must interpret these parables in connection with the whole Gospel, we must understand the urgency of the warning in this case. Because the time is short and because the message of Jesus claims to be God's last word before the end, the warning is to be taken more seriously than in any other case: it is the last hour; you must repent if you want to be saved!

In considering the formal similarities and the real differences between the Jewish tradition and the sayings of Jesus we meet another problem which our examination of the Sermon on the Mount has not yet solved: what is the relation of the Sermon on the Mount to the Old Testament and its Law?

A direct relation to the Old Testament is expressed in the introductory formula: "You have heard that it was said to the men of old time . . . but I say unto you . . . " This introduction is used for the first time in Jesus' enlarged interpretation of the sixth commandment which we examined above only in connection with the Gospel and not in its relation to the law. The content of that interpretation of the law is as follows: the punishment which, according to Moses, is meted out for murder should be applied for anger as well; and for a slight insult as, *e.g.*, "silly ass" (*raca*) a still more severe punishment by the Sanhedrin, the High Court of Justice, is in order, while the grave offender who says "you fool" shall be liable to hell fire.

At first sight one might think that all that is implied here is a more severe system of punishment. But this interpretation would be wrong because the saying makes no provision to apply a commensurate punishment to the gravest of crimes, like manslaughter and murder. There is no punishment more severe than that of hell fire, and it is visited upon him who merely says "you fool" (in the sense of "scoundrel"; it must be worse than "stupid"). It should be clear that the whole arrangement working up to a climax must have a symbolic value. The meaning of this passage, therefore, is, that those who want to fulfil the sixth commandment are forbidden to become angry and to use invectives and, by so much the more, also, to commit any acts of violence.

Jesus cites the Old Testament commandment "thou shalt not kill"—for the benefit of God's children— merely as an example of God's intention. The pure will of God demands more. It forbids even the beginning of the criminal urge. It is quite the same in the case of adultery. Whoever looks on a woman (a married woman of course, for the question at issue is the violation of marriage) to desire her has committed adultery with her. God regards desire as though it had become action; the lascivious glance is only one form of desire. In this connection we may recall what Jesus said concerning the oath. The Jewish Law forbids perjury. We learn from Jesus that every oath is a kind of perjury, because we are not entitled to name anything in the world as warrant of our trustworthiness, for all things belong to God and we are not allowed to dispose of the disposer of all.

Jesus is speaking to a people who live under the Law. The Jews have in the Old Testament the historic revelation of God's demand, shaped in regard to the hardness of their own hearts. But the true children of the coming Kingdom must consider more than the wording of the Old Testament commandments. They must recognize what is the full intention of God, His pure and absolute will.

Jesus speaks of the customs of Jewish piety in quite the same way. The question is not whether they will still exist in the Kingdom of God. His Jewish hearers who want to be children of the coming Kingdom are obliged to observe the customs of their traditional piety in accordance with God's ultimate purpose. Jesus' position on this point is clear; he desires that such acts of piety should not be mere outward performances done before men, but acts of man's faith, done before God alone, without any claim or pretension.

Such pretensions as Jewish piety really has are described by Jesus in the hyperbolic manner of the Orient; he speaks of the hypocrites who sound a trumpet before themselves when they give alms, who stand on the corners of the street when they pray, who look gloomy so that men may notice their fasting and praise their piety. The commands which Jesus gives are couched in the same language and are therefore also hyperbolic. "When you fast, you should anoint your head and wash your face," *i.e.*, you should act as if you were going to dinner. We do not suggest that Jesus in attempting to combat Jewish hypocrisy would recommend only a new kind of deception. He wants to characterize the true attitude of the man who is fasting, not before men, but only before God. If this is true, we must interpret the rules concerning other pious customs in the same way. This holds true for the commandment on prayer: "If you pray, enter your chamber and shut your door." This is, of course, a metaphorical description of an unpretentious prayer, a prayer before God alone. That the rule about the true almsgiving—"let not thy left hand know what thy right hand doeth"—is metaphorical too, we scarcely need to prove.

We are now in a position to summarize what the substance and purpose of Jesus' interpretation of the Old Testament Law and of Jewish piety really is. The Jewish people have their traditional rules of conduct. Jesus says to them: "These rules can reveal to you the will of God if you regard them, not as a literal, complete description of that will, but rather as the means and the occasion of ascertaining its basic character and purpose. You must go farther than the words of the Law. You must not restrict yourselves to the fulfilment of the written commandments. Whoever is truly intent upon God and His Kingdom and not only upon the wording of the Law, will deepen the significance of the commandments and expand their validity."

Once we have understood Jesus' attitude to the Law, we can understand the words with which the several sayings about the individual commandments are introduced in the Sermon on the Mount. According to the method of Form-Criticism, we were to consider first of all the special sayings which follow

Matthew 5:21, and not that general introduction, for we may suppose that the tradition of the special sayings is an old one and a trustworthy one. But as regards this introductory section we must suppose that the whole paragraph has been put together by the author of the Gospel of Matthew, and that he collected some words of Jesus and perhaps other sayings in order to form a general interpretation of the new law which follows. Indeed, these introductory words embrace some conservative sayings: "Till heaven and earth pass away, one jot or tittle shall in no wise pass away from the law" and "Every one who declares even one of these least commandments invalid and teaches men so, shall be called least in the Kingdom of Heaven," etc. It may be that some of these words are insertions or at least corrections which reflect the attitude of certain conservative Christian communities rather than the attitude of our Lord. The main thought of this introductory section, however, is in accordance with the interpretation of the special commandments we have just considered. The basic point of view finds expression in two words:

(1) "Unless your righteousness exceeds the righteousness of the Scribes and Pharisees, you shall in no wise enter in the Kingdom of Heaven." This passage gives expression to the new extension and deepening of the individual rules which Jesus teaches in order to give examples of the pure will of God. It gives expression to the radicalism of the Gospel, not a rigid radicalism such as Stoics teach, but a radicalism de-

termined by the proximity of the Kingdom. In the face of the coming crisis the disciples of Jesus are obliged to take the will of God seriously, more seriously than the Scribes did.

(2) The second saying of determinative character in this introductory section is: "Think not that I came to destroy the law or the prophets; I came not to destroy, but to fulfil" (Matt. 5:17). The contradiction between destroy and fulfil shows clearly that the meaning of "fulfil" is not simply "to do." Far from wishing to abolish the Old Testament or the Jewish customs Jesus actually aims at deepening and extending their significance. His task is to reveal the true will of God hidden in the wording of the Law. What he proclaims is not a change in the Law but rather a change in the attitude of man. His followers are not to make the literal performance of the entire Law the supreme purpose of their lives. Rather, they are to seek to ascertain the true will of God, as we have already seen. Of this will the individual commandments are only examples, but as examples they are accurate and significant.

Again the eschatological background of Jesus' message becomes visible. In view of the coming of the Kingdom it is not important to abolish the Law or to change the commandments or the pious customs. There is no reason why Jesus should insist upon the newness of all his sayings. He is absolutely free to use sayings of popular wisdom, not because they are traditional—as the Scribes did—but because they reveal

the will of God. We have already found some examples of popular sayings in the Sermon on the Mount,
the golden rule and the isolated saying Matthew 6:34
"take no thought for the morrow," etc. Exegesis was
often wrong in emphasizing the statement that every
genuine saying of Jesus must be a new one. What is
actually new is not in any case the wording but the
background, the nearness of the Kingdom. Therefore it does not matter, if in the future scholars should
discover more parallels to the sayings of our Lord in
Jewish or Hellenistic tradition than we possess at
the present. For in comparison with such parallels
the sayings of the Sermon on the Mount would have
a new urgency in connection with the proclamation of
the coming Kingdom. They would express the new
attitude of man toward God.

The best example, perhaps, of this new attitude in
the Sermon on the Mount is the Lord's Prayer. In
view of God's Kingdom prayer has a new urgency
as the expression of man's trust in God's grace and not
merely as the fulfilment of God's demand. Therefore, children of the Kingdom should not address
their father before men (Matt. 6:5). To this urgency
there is a corresponding certainty that God hears
prayer as expressed in Matthew 7:7: "Ask, and it shall
be given you." A pattern of the content of prayer is
given by the Lord's Prayer in Matthew 6:9 and Luke
11:2.

It is a pattern, originally, and not a formula. Jesus
did not give to his hearers formulas for worship, but

rather an example of the new attitude of man. It was not his task to improve worship in itself. He wanted to proclaim what and how children of the coming Kingdom should pray. The Lord's Prayer is not exhaustive and does not cover the whole field of human needs and requirements; a formula, of course, would have to be as exhaustive as possible. The Lord's Prayer is not so original that a Jew of Jesus' time could not have prayed in the same way, using the same words.

Already in the early time of the Church there was a tendency to complete the Lord's Prayer by inserting a petition that God may grant His Holy Spirit to those who are praying. This insertion is found in Luke in a smaller group of manuscripts which substitutes the following for the first or second petition: "Thy Holy Spirit come over us and make us clean." The reason for this insertion is probably the desire to have a petition in the Lord's Prayer which is specifically Christian. Indeed, the petition for the Holy Spirit is characteristic of the Christian community and marks a difference between the Christians and the Jews as well as between our Lord's disciples and John the Baptist's. But this desire for originality did not concern our Lord.

The text of the Lord's Prayer is not the same in Matthew and Luke. In Luke, according to our best manuscripts, the third and the seventh petitions are missing, *i.e.*, the words "Thy will be done," etc., as well as "Deliver us from evil." It is difficult to imagine that somebody has removed these petitions. On the contrary, it seems probable that Christian communities have inserted both petitions in order to get a full Seven-Petition-Prayer for their service, which, perhaps, they wanted to have in accordance with Psalm 119:164, "Seven times a day do I praise thee." Therefore, when we consider the original meaning of our Lord's Prayer we should deal with the short text as we read it in Luke according to the best manuscripts.

The next problem before us is the meaning of the first petition: "Hallowed be thy name." Conceivably this petition might deal with the sanctification of the divine name by words and deeds everywhere. But we must recall that in Luke there is no specific address at the beginning of the prayer except the one word "Father." It is a custom of Jewish piety not to name God without some expression of reverence (cf. the usual rabbinic title of God in the Talmud, "The Holy One, blessed be He"). Therefore, it seems probable that this so-called first petition in the original text belongs to the introduction and that the beginning of the prayer runs as follows: "Father, Thy Holy name be sanctified" (be blessed). The last words of the prayer, "Lead us not into temptation," which in the original text as handed down by Luke form not the seventh but the sixth petition, require similar treatment. Construed as a separate element of the whole they are awkward because they do not have the character of a closing sentence. Hence it is better to interpret them as a part of the petition for forgiveness, and to paraphrase this petition: "Forgive us our sins and protect us from sins in the future," *i.e.*, on every occasion when we are tempted to sin.

Now we are in a position to interpret the whole text of the prayer in the original wording. There are three great petitions which the disciple of Jesus should bring before God's throne. He should ask for the coming of the Kingdom, for his daily bread and for forgiveness of his sins in the past as well as in the future. The first and the last of these petitions are understandable in themselves. The petition for bread embraces the disciple's livelihood and—we may add— all things which he needs during his earthly existence. They are not to be mentioned verbally, for "your heavenly Father knows that ye have need of all these things." Those who are expecting the Kingdom have in the present age, during the time between the times, no other needs than the Kingdom of Heaven, the earthly life and God's forgiving grace.

Here a comparison with other forms of prayer seems to be worthy of consideration. Hellenistic theology developed a theory of mysticism which states that it is not in accordance with God's dignity to be concerned with human needs. Consequently, the only fitting prayer is one of thanksgiving. Through praise man gives back to God what he has received from Him, whether the gift received be interpreted as grace or shining light or divine essence. Man as such is entirely incapable of offering suitable prayers to God.

The best evidence of such a conception we find in

the so-called Hermetic writings, those mystic texts originating in the first centuries of the Christian era which represent a pious devotion of a mystic and sometimes gnostic type, the devotion, perhaps, of particular communities or of intimate groups. Here we find in the so-called *Asclepius* (Pseudo-Apuleius, *Asclepius* 41) a warning against the use of incense. "Such gifts as these are unfit for him; for he is filled with all things that exist and lacks nothing. Let us adore him rather with thanksgiving; for words of praise are the only offering that he accepts" (translation by Walter Scott, *Hermetica* I, 373). Sometimes a still deeper mysticism forbids every kind of oral prayer and allows only silence as the most fitting kind of worship; "for the knowledge of God is deep (?) silence and suppression of all the senses" (*Corpus Herm.* 10, 5).

This Hellenistic concept has also influenced Christian ideas of prayer in the early Church. But this is by no means the idea of prayer in the mind of Jesus. He teaches his disciples to speak frankly to their heavenly Father. Naturally, a man who is waiting for the coming Kingdom must put at the beginning of his prayer the petition for its coming, but he ventures to bring before God his own cares also. He prays with full reverence for God's majesty but also with full trust in God's grace. Prayer is no longer a sacrifice which man offers, as it was in antiquity; it is rather an expression of man's attitude toward God. It is the same, when the Apostle Paul prays "in Christ," not because he takes this position only for the moment of prayer, but because he lives and acts continually "in Christ."

Here the difference between the attitude of the Jew to his Law and the attitude of the disciple to the law of God's Kingdom becomes visible. To the message of God's Kingdom man is to be transformed. He knows that he belongs to God; he knows that God claims his obedience. This obedience concerns not only some single rules but the totality of his life. God demands more than that man should perform some particular commandments; He demands that man become a new being, living under the eyes of God and in the consciousness of His will. This new attitude, this overcoming of the old obedience toward the Law by a new one, has its origin in the message of the coming Kingdom. This message guarantees the unity of all particular demands in the Gospel, especially in the Sermon on the Mount. They are no longer single commandments, but examples and expressions of God's total claim.

Therefore when Christians speak of a new law revealed by Christ, especially in the Sermon on the Mount, this does not mean that the old Jewish Law is replaced by a new one or completed by some more severe rules. It means that man lives in a new dependence upon God's will and wants to perform it. As examples he uses the Sermon on the Mount and other commandments of the Gospel, but he does not use them as the Scribes used the Jewish Law and the Stoics used the "law of nature." He does not use the

Sermon on the Mount in order to justify or to criticize the deeds of men.

The method of judging human conduct by the standard of the Law is abolished by the revelation of the divine will. For Christ has brought with him not the revelation of a new law but the message of the Kingdom. Its purpose is to transform men, and a transformed humanity will be able to do more than men did under the government of the old Law. Man will recognize the will of God in every situation, even if the commandments of the Bible do not cover this situation. In this way a transformed man is able to know more of the divine will than Israel did, and to do more than the Law requires, because he is instructed by Jesus' examples of the divine will and by his announcement of the heavenly Kingdom. Thus, in proclaiming the absolute will of God, Jesus speaks not as a legislator, but as God's ambassador in the last hour. He comes to announce the Kingdom of Heaven and, perhaps, to inaugurate it.

Here we meet the great christological problem. Who is the man who is allowed to speak with divine authority, with messianic authority? What is the significance of the Sermon on the Mount in relation to the Messiahship of Jesus? We shall deal with this problem in the next chapter.

CHAPTER VI

The Sermon on the Mount and Christ's Mission

WE SAW that the question of legalism broadens out to include the christological question, namely: what is the importance of the Sermon on the Mount in relation to Jesus' Messiahship? With this question we must now concern ourselves. A christological question—can such a question really arise from a consideration of the Sermon on the Mount? Perhaps some theologians of the older generation would reply that the Sermon on the Mount raises no christological issue whatsoever. They might contend that it contains only some sayings and words of wisdom, of divine wisdom of course, spoken by a rabbi in Galilee. This rabbi was an ambassador of God, they might continue, perhaps the definitive ambassador, and for this reason he speaks with great authority. But his manner of expressing his opinion does not in any way reveal a claim to authority higher than this. The Sermon on the Mount implies that Jesus has the right to speak thus; but there is no hint that he wants to be something more than an inspired teacher of wisdom.

Thus one might say the Sermon on the Mount gives evidence of a stage in early Christian history, when Christianity had not yet developed any definite christological idea. This opinion which I have briefly characterized is promulgated in many circles. At the beginning of this century, Adolf Harnack, the greatest among the German historians of Christianity, formulated this opinion as follows: in the Gospel which Jesus preaches only the Father and not the Son finds a place. In a sense, we must confess, this view is correct, especially so in regard to the Sermon on the Mount. The Sermon on the Mount, it is true, does not have a strongly marked christology. This is not, however, a full answer to our question.

Alongside this first observation we must place a second one, perhaps no less crucial than the first. Many of the words spoken by Jesus have parallels in the older Jewish literature or in the writings of the Jewish rabbis. Perhaps we may venture to say that if we knew more of these Jewish sayings, we should have still more parallels. Perhaps only the most radical of the sayings of the Sermon on the Mount would remain absolutely unique. On the other hand no rabbinic pronouncement ever became authoritative for the world outside Judaism. Only the relatively small group of sayings collected in the Sermon on the Mount has won authority for millions of men. This has happened only because it was Jesus who proclaimed these sayings. The Sermon on the Mount is not an arbitrary collection of sayings, but it is Christ's own Gospel, and only as such has it achieved and does it maintain its authority for the

Christians. Therefore we must confess that there *is* a christological question in the Sermon on the Mount.

To solve the problem thus raised I propose to make a distinction between the time in which Jesus lived and the time when the sayings were collected, *i.e.*, between the situation *before Easter* and the situation *after Easter*.

Let us briefly characterize the situation prevailing before Easter. Jesus proclaimed his message in Galilee at different occasions to different groups of people, but always with the same intent, namely, to proclaim the absolute will of God and to announce the Kingdom of Heaven. According to the Synoptists it would seem that Jesus did not say anything about his own authority or Messiahship, at least he did not do so as a rule.

Open-minded New Testament criticism finds the interpretation of the Gospel passages dealing with Christ's Messiahship very difficult. From the historical point of view most of them are open to serious doubt. The story of Peter's confession is a case in point. According to Mark and Luke, when Peter confesses Jesus as the Messiah, he does not receive an affirmative answer. Instead Jesus merely forbids the disciples to publish their knowledge of his Messiahship. Only Matthew relates the famous answer which praises Peter, as the one who has received this revelation from God; and according to Matthew, and Matthew alone, Jesus continues: "And now I say to thee that thou art Peter and upon this rock I will build my Church; and the

gates of hell shall not prevail against it." The question
arises why these words are not recorded in the other
Gospels as well. Perhaps the best reply is that this
passage is not a part of the original story. From the
historical point of view the answer which Jesus gives
to the High Priest during the trial before the Sanhedrin may be doubted too. For it is probable that the
Christian congregations did not have at their disposal
an eye-witness who could report to them that Jesus
said: "I am," meaning, I am the Messiah, as we are
told in Mark 14:62.

But perhaps Form-Criticism can protect us from a
radical scepticism on this point. It is the supposition
of Form-Criticism that the tradition handed down in
the Synoptic Gospels was formulated in terms of the
Christian faith and for the requirements of this faith.
Therefore it is quite natural that all allusions of our
Lord to his Messiahship were transformed by the
Evangelists into Christian confessions in the time after
Easter. Hence we have no real reason to draw a scep-
tical conclusion from the fact that the relevant passages
express Christian convictions, and it is not necessary
to take for granted that Jesus did not make any allusions to his Messiahship at all. It is probable, rather,
that the question who would be the King of the coming
Kingdom was before his followers during his lifetime
and that his listeners had at least a vague impression
of their Master's higher authority.

At any rate, his disciples "forsook all and followed
him," not because he uttered impressive sayings, like

a wise rabbi, but because they believed that in connection with his work the Kingdom of God would appear on earth. We do not know how many of his followers used the word "Messiah" to express their hope of the coming of the Kingdom. But the execution of Jesus as King of the Jews seems to prove that a rumour about his Messiahship influenced the procedure of his enemies. It is difficult to imagine that incidents like the entry into Jerusalem or the cleansing of the temple could have occurred without awakening, either among friends or enemies, the presentiment of his Messiahship. In the opinion of his disciples Jesus was the warrant of the Kingdom; his healings and his sayings were the *signs* that the Kingdom was at hand.

The best evidence we have for the significance of the healings, as well as of the sayings, is Jesus' answer to the Baptist's question: "Art thou the Coming One or are we to look for another?" Jesus gives no affirmative answer to this personal question but he directs attention to what is happening about him. The healings which he performs give evidence, if not of the Coming One, at least of the coming Kingdom. All that Jesus says about himself is: "Blessed is he whosoever shall not be offended in me." His principal demand is that the Baptist should believe in the Kingdom and should recognize his deeds and healings as signs of its imminent advent. He does not require of men that they apply messianic or other honorific titles to him; he merely wishes that his listeners should not be prevented by his personal behaviour from believing in the Kingdom and from understanding his healings as signs of the Kingdom.

This explains why Jesus' healings have the character of acts done at random. Jesus did not cure all those among his people who were ill, and it is a great mistake to regard Jesus essentially as a great miracle-worker and his mission as a medical one. How many sick men lived in Palestine in Jesus' day and how few were those who were cured by the Saviour! He wanted to give evidence by his healings of heavenly powers and to convince people of the reality of these powers, and thus of the nearness of the Kingdom. He desired to impress upon those he healed that by God's grace they were admitted into discipleship. From the fact of their being healed they may infer that God will have mercy upon their soul also. "Son, thy sins be forgiven thee." Then, blessed and pardoned by God's grace, they are obliged to change their sinful life: "Go and sin no more." The healings performed by Jesus are thus to be interpreted as a part of his preaching, as an announcement of the coming change, as signs of the heavenly Kingdom.

This holds good for the *sayings* of Jesus too. His exhortations and decisions did not cover the whole field of human activity. He did not solve all prob-lems of this life and did not arbitrate all conflicts of the world. We remember his word in Luke (12:14): "Man, who made me a judge or an arbitrator over you?" Finally, he did not try to win the whole population of his country. He spoke to the people who came to listen; according to our sources he abstained from all manner of public propaganda. It would be quite in harmony with our findings to construe even the sayings of Jesus as signs of the coming Kingdom. We saw in the last chapters that his commandments did not form a law adapted to conditions in this world, but a law of God's Kingdom, a proclamation of the divine will without any regard for the earthly circumstances and the daily life of men. This proclamation nonetheless gives to the listeners the presentiment of the imminent coming of God. Therefore we may actually call the sayings of Jesus signs of the Kingdom.

This is in accordance with Jesus' own utterances. We remember all the eschatological sayings recorded by Luke in the second half of his twelfth chapter. In this context we read the warning: "Ye hypocrites, ye can discern the face of the sky and of the earth, but how is it that ye do not discern this time" (*i.e.*, the signs of the last hour)? Here we find also the saying of the watching servants: "Blessed are those servants, whom the Lord when he comes shall find watching." The preaching of Jesus was really intended to awaken men by a sign from heaven, but not in the usual sense of a miraculous sign. Thus, these sayings of Jesus had a different influence upon his listeners than the wise words of the teachers, philosophers or prophets. Similarly, the sayings which we read in the Sermon on the Mount had a higher validity for the disciples than the word of the Scribes, for Jesus spoke with a higher authority than did the Scribes. He spoke as "one having authority." In summarizing all these considerations we may say that his personal conduct on the whole seemed to be a warrant of the Kingdom.

I am not inclined to attach great importance to the question whether Jesus in his personal life was able to avoid adapting his actions to the circumstances of this life. Notice, for instance, that we do not know whether Jesus used the oath in connection with his trial before the High Priest. Indeed, we do not know whether the question of his judge actually took the form given by Matthew, and Matthew alone, namely: "I adjure thee by the living God, that thou tell us whether thou be the Christ, the Son of God." Even if this form had been used and if the answer to this question had had the validity of an oath, the compulsion exerted by the circumstances of the trial, taking place in this age, would have no bearing upon the proclamation of the will of God as expressed in the Sermon on the Mount in the words: "I say unto you, swear not at all!" That is: the conditions of the life of Jesus are not the conditions of the Kingdom of God. Therefore the discussion of the question whether Jesus may, or may not, have been able to bring all incidents of his life into harmony with the law of the Kingdom is not very fruitful. We are dealing here with possibilities only. But even if he had not been able to do so, this would not have any bearing upon our problem, and thus make it necessary for us to take the Sermon on the Mount in a less absolute sense.

From this consideration we may draw two conclusions. First, we are not allowed to interpret the Sermon on the Mount according to any incidents or circumstances of the life of Jesus, as is often done. Second, we cannot solve the christological problem of the Sermon on the Mount by saying that Jesus, and Jesus alone, personally fulfilled the commandments of this sermon in his life. At least, this point of view is in no way emphasized by the New Testament texts. The Sermon on the Mount makes demands too exacting to be fulfilled in life on this earth, even in the life of the Saviour himself, for his life was bound by earthly circumstances too. The impression we have from the New Testament is rather this: whatever may have·happened during Jesus' life, he was for his followers the personal embodiment of the coming Kingdom; he.proclaimed its law by words, he gave a foretaste of its power by his healings, he inaugurated the new age.

Let us now consider the other situation, the situation *after Easter*, in which the state of affairs was completely changed. The origin of the Christian community is the conviction that Jesus did not remain in the grave, that God raised him from the dead, and that the risen and exalted Christ will return and bring from heaven the divine Kingdom. For this reason, from the point of view of the first Christians the last great time of crisis has already begun. The Christians

are waiting for the coming of their Lord. Consequently, all commandments of Jesus handed down to
the communities assume the character of a testament.
The Christians feel that Christ has instructed them to
live in accordance with these sayings. They are not any
longer proclamations of the will of God in all its
radicalism; they become rules of conduct for the life
within the communities and are adapted to the conditions of this life. They are no longer single sayings
spoken at different occasions and to different people.
They are brought together and codified to form systems of ordinances like the new law laid down in the
Sermon on the Mount. This was possible only because
the words of the Sermon on the Mount had been
spoken by the Messiah, the Christ, the Lord, the Son
of God.

What the early Christian communities wanted was
not a collection of maxims—even though they might
be very valuable maxims—and not in the first instance
an impressive preaching; they needed a testament of
their Lord, the revelation of the living Christ in their
own midst. The tradition of the sayings takes a recognized place in the communities alongside the manifestations of the Holy Spirit; both are indications of
the exalted Christ and of the coming Kingdom. Whoever doubted whether the new age had actually begun
was to be convinced by the gifts of the Holy Ghost,
such as the gifts of speaking, of teaching, of prophesy-
ing, of healing, and the miraculous capacity of search-
ing one's heart. Whoever did not know how to live in

this world was to be informed by the words of the
Lord, by their radicalism and by their authority.

Here we notice the correspondence between the
first hearers of Jesus and the early Christian communities, between the believers before Easter and
after Easter. Both are convinced that Jesus has the
right to speak as he does, because he knows the will of
God; and he has this knowledge not as a priest, as the
professional representative of God in the world, not
as a scribe who reveals divine secrets as the fruit of
scholarly study, but he has this knowledge as the ambassador of God who brings the message of His will.
Thus, in the time before Easter some people felt that
he was the man whom God would choose to be the
ruler of the coming Kingdom, the Messiah. In hearing his words they took them not as wise sayings but
as an authoritative message from God. In the time
after Easter all Christian people knew and were convinced that Jesus was the Lord, exalted in order to
bring the Kingdom from heaven, and in reading his
words they took them as the decisive revelation from
God. Matthew expresses this thought in the word
which serves as an epilogue to the Sermon on the
Mount: "he taught them as one having authority."
Similarly in John's Gospel we read: "I have declared
unto them thy name and will declare it" (John
17:26). In Paul's First Epistle to the Corinthians we
hear of "Christ Jesus who of God was made unto us
wisdom and righteousness and sanctification and redemption" (I Cor. 1:30). This christological convic-

tion expressed in different terms is the common link
which binds together the presentiment of the disciples
before Easter and the faith of the Christians after
Easter.

In quoting these words from so many different
early Christian writings we meet the greatest problem
of the whole New Testament. This problem is determined by the difference of the two halves of the New
Testament, that is, in broadest outline, the difference
between the Epistles and the Gospels. It seems at first
sight that the Epistles do not tell anything about the
earthly life of Christ but rather give evidence of his
divine authority—and that the Gospels are not written
from a special christological point of view, but rather
to tell the history of Jesus' life and of his passion.
Those who have a deeper understanding of the whole
New Testament must affirm that there is a relation
between the two groups of writings, for words of a
christological character do appear in the Gospels and
allusions to the historical record are to be found in the
Epistles. The supreme witness of the relationship is
the Gospel of John, which actually combines history
and christology. The author of John's Gospel uses
the record of Jesus' earthly life to show his heavenly
glory. What Mark ventured to represent only in one
unique scene—the story of the transfiguration—namely
that the teacher of Galilee is a heavenly figure, is
actually the theme of the Fourth Gospel. Nevertheless, the impression of a great difference within the
New Testament is basically correct; in spite of these

elements which join the two halves together, the gap exists, and we must not bridge it by overemphasizing what the two parts have in common.

No, we must seek another solution of the problem. To find it we must go back once more and give full value to the eschatological situation, to the position of the first Christian communities between the two ages. For the first Christians the old age is practically at an end, thanks to God's interference; the new age is coming and the signs of its coming on earth are the manifestations of the Holy Spirit and the existence of the Christian community. This eschatological faith, the main element in the consciousness of the Christian community, lives on and is strengthened by the knowledge, that God has spoken His definitive word, has done His decisive deed, has given His only-begotten Son. The historical fact that the Christ had lived on earth in the immediate past established the conviction that God has already begun the great transformation of the world. It guaranteed the hope that the same Christ, who had lived as a man in a Galilean family and then moved in a wider circle in intercourse with his disciples and other people, would shortly come back as the Lord.

The historical Jesus is thus also the Lord of the Christian faith. The eschatological preaching of the Epistles is founded in the Gospel, which tell of the happenings inaugurating the eschatological era. Thus eschatology provides the connection between the two halves of the New Testament. For this reason we are able to quote, as I did, words from various parts of the New Testament to characterize the christological authority of the Sermon on the Mount. Whatever the messianic presentiment of the people was who listened to the sayings of Jesus during his life, for those who collected these sayings the preacher on the Mount was obviously the Messiah, in whom all Christians believed. And it was thought evident that the content of the earthly life of the Messiah could only be the standard of Christian conduct till his return.

Now we understand why the Christian communities needed to have both a summary of Jesus' deeds, and a collection of his principal sayings. This double requirement is the starting point of *the formation of Gospel Tradition*. It was formulated as oral or written tradition during the first decades after Jesus' death. It was handed down to the preachers and teachers, completed and enlarged, and finally collected in books of rather popular style. The result of this process were the texts which we call Gospels. No doubt there were many similar books in the different communities, and Luke is right in emphasizing that many have undertaken to construct a narrative of those things which were accomplished among the men of Palestine around the year 30 of the Christian era. The comparison of these books, stimulated by a process of critical evaluation going on within the Church, brought into existence the authoritative collection of the four Gospels in the second half of the second century.

The decision reached by the Church in this matter

is very important. These Christians of the second century were so interested in the old tradition (*i.e.*, in history), that they did not venture to authorize a new book, such a book as Tatian's *Harmony of the Four Gospels*, but preferred to preserve the books containing the old tradition. The privileged position accorded to the three traditional Gospels, Matthew, Mark and Luke, had as a consequence the abolition of certain other books, *e.g.*, the Gospel a fragment of which was recently published by Bell and Skeat (Pap. Egerton, no. 2). Probably the standard of selection was not the historical value of the books but rather their use in the principal communities. Indeed, the abolished books were not at all heretical, but harmless texts, used only in smaller circles. The Church was so interested in a deeper understanding of the revelation in Christ, that to the three traditional Gospels a "modern" book was added as a fourth, namely the Gospel of John. I call it a modern book because its contents are a part of the tradition, elaborated in modern, more or less Hellenistic idiom. This statement an inference from the authorship of the book. The fact that John's Gospel is in this sense a modern book must be acknowledged without regard to the question of the authorship. Again we notice the interest of the old communities, both in history and christology.

The connection between this whole process and the Christian faith becomes clear when we bear in mind the manifold possibilities and requirements of the Christian preaching. Early Christian preaching involved first the proclamation that the Word of God was made flesh, that God revealed Himself in a human being. In connection with this the Christian preacher found it necessary to relate incidents from the historical life of Jesus. In the second place Christian preaching uttered the call to repentance. It proclaimed that the Kingdom of God is at hand; and that men must turn back from the way of sin. For this the preachers needed a statement about the will of God; and the most important of the sayings of Jesus were used as proclamations of this will. Finally the preachers had to admonish the Christians with regard to their future conduct—and for this purpose they used other sayings of Jesus, sayings which criticized daily life and gave instruction for a life according to the will of God.

Now we recognize the practical need of the communities for a collection of prophetical sayings as well as for a summary of Jesus' wisdom. Now we understand too that the communities took the words of the Sermon on the Mount not as the law of the coming Kingdom but as practicable ordinances for the Christian life. Now we see finally why it was possible and sometimes necessary to alter the wording of the sayings (cf. p. 18). The Christians needed the words of Christ in a practical form; therefore some accommodations to the practical necessities of life were inevitable. The sayings of the Sermon on the Mount were originally meant in an absolute sense, but as a law for the coming Kingdom rather than as a law governing life in this world. Their practicability for the workaday life was therefore originally restricted. The Christians undertook to alter and adapt them in order to make them more directly applicable to the circumstances of this life.

In the second and in the fourth chapters I mentioned some examples of such alterations. Here I add a passage from the period after the writing of the Gospels; it contains two most convincing examples. I refer to the *Didache*, the old Church order book written in the second Christian century, the first part of which probably has an earlier origin. In this part the well-known commandment to love one's enemy has the form: "love them who hate you, then you will have no enemies." Here, indeed, the heroic command of Jesus reproduced in the Sermon on the Mount has undergone an utilitarian transformation. The other commandment of the Sermon on the Mount not to resist aggression by force here reads as follows: "and from him who takes away your goods ask them not again; neither will you be able to do so." This addition seems to be more clever than Christian. The meaning is that the poor and powerless people in the first communities cannot possibly obtain full restitution in the case of aggression, therefore to the author of this addition it seems better to remain silent rather than to fight against a violent adversary.

To understand this whole method of adapting Jesus' words we must bear in mind two things. The first is that in the opinion of the Christian it involved no falsification. These sayings were the expression of the will of God, and if a man understood the will of God better than others had before him, so that he was able to adapt this expression to the requirements of a workaday life, then with God's help by the Holy Spirit it was permitted him to do anything which might make the saying useful for a better understanding of God's will.

The second thing to bear in mind, a thing which I should like to emphasize more than it is usually emphasized today, is that the Christians of those days expected the end of the world in the near future. For this reason such alterations as they undertook had only a limited validity. The end of the world would soon come, and then in the new world the will of God alone would be of value. Whatever has been altered for the short span of the present life will be forgotten. Hence it is not a sin to adapt the words of Jesus to the circumstances of the present day. The shortness of the time limits the validity of the change, and the word is thus made subject to the conditions which determine the life of the Christian in this world generally. Christian people stand between two ages. On the one hand they are still subject to the conditions of this life and on the other hand they know the pure will of God and are waiting for the time when this will shall be fully realized. This position of the Christians between the two ages in a way legitimizes the transformation of the Sermon on the Mount into a practical law for the Christian conduct on earth.

Now we are in a position to give a summary of what we may call the theological character of the Sermon on the Mount.

(1) Let us start with the question of its practicability. The sayings of the Sermon on the Mount reveal the pure will of God and therefore must be fulfilled. There are certain exceptions to this; namely those sayings which are given in the form of hyperbole. Such hyperbolic sayings are to guide men in the direction of the coming Kingdom. They are not adequate descriptions of human conduct, but for the members of the first Christian communities there was no danger of any mistake in this point. People of the ancient Orient were accustomed to that manner of speaking in hyperbolic expressions. They felt the right meaning behind the wording and did not need any explanation. With this exception the sayings are to be regarded as practicable, just as the pure will of God must be considered practicable. Only it must be remembered that the application of these sayings is limited so far as the present age is concerned. The performance of the pure will of God is in the present world, consequently hindered. The real fulfilment of this great Christian law is possible only in the Kingdom of God.

(2) We consider next the question of eschatology. Because they are a revelation of the divine will, the sayings of the Sermon on the Mount have an eschatological significance. They are the law of the Kingdom. But much as we owe to Albert Schweitzer for his

eschatological interpretations of the Gospels, we dare
not follow him in construing them as the expression
of an "interim-ethic." These commandments were
given not for the short time intervening between the
present and the end of the world. They were given for
eternity, because they represent the will of the eternal
God. Therefore we may call all of them eschatological
sayings, not only those which speak expressly of the
coming world, but all the commandments in the Gospel, for their starting point is the will of God, not
human ability. Their standard is the existence of the
coming world, not our human life within earthly circumstances. Those who want to be children of the
Kingdom even now, during this age, are obliged to
live their lives in obedience to the will of God. This
is the practical implication of what Paul means when
he speaks of being "in Christ." To be "in Christ" and
to possess his Holy Spirit means to participate in the
coming world and internally to be free from the
earthly circumstances. Thus, the eschatological supposition enables the preacher on the Mount to speak as
he does without any consideration of the conditions of
this age.

(3) If we take the Sermon on the Mount as the
representation of God's will we must recognize that
full obedience here and now is impossible. We ought
to be honest enough to confess our inability in this
matter. The first communities felt these difficulties
too, for they moderated and accommodated the radical
commandments of the Sermon on the Mount to the

needs of daily life, as we have seen. Modern theologians have often tried to achieve the same purpose by scientific interpretation, but we have no right to let ourselves be deceived by certain methods of interpretation. Only a superficial interpretation can so overestimate the eschatological character of the Sermon on the Mount as to suppose that the fulfilment of its commandments must be postponed until the coming age. For Jesus spoke to me of this present age. If we realize as we should that he addressed the sayings of the Sermon on the Mount to different people on various occasions, it seems impossible to imagine that his commandments did not concern the present in which he lived. Actually they were spoken to awaken his listeners, to thrill them, to stimulate them and, I venture to say, to offend them.

It would be superficial, too, to exaggerate the hyperbolic character of the Oriental style, thereby to limit the validity of the Sermon on the Mount in its main points and to transform it into a set of rules expressing a very moderate ideal. The Oriental hyperbole is only a method of sharpening certain sayings; their rigidness must not be put aside by the statement that they are hyperbolic. No, the method of interpretation to which we must give preference is that which will grieve and offend our natural feelings. Jesus came not to bring peace but a sword, and to set a man at variance with his father and mother.

Thus, we come face to face with our last question in this field, the question what the Sermon on the Mount meant to those who heard it, standing as they believed in the period immediately preceding the end of the world. I am not speaking here of the significance of the Sermon on the Mount for the modern world. This will be the subject of the last chapter. My concern here is with Jesus' hearers and disciples.

The Sermon on the Mount is not a system either of ethics or of dogmatics. It does not cover the whole field of human conduct, either in the present or in the past. The sayings proclaimed the declared will of God only with respect to certain matters. If we were to extend the content of the Sermon on the Mount so as to cover the whole of life, and imagine a set of sayings equally radical in character, governing all occasions, we would construct a revolutionary law, the fulfilment of which would throw the whole world into turmoil. But it was not Jesus' purpose to give such a law to the world of his day. His task was another. We must look at his own attitude to understand what he regarded as his mission.

We have seen already that Jesus did not act as one who is an agitator for his own cause and who is obliged to win as many followers as he can. He chose a small number of disciples, a nucleus of the coming Kingdom, and a circle of faithful adherents who were waiting for this Kingdom. When he left his native country Galilee to go to Jerusalem, he did not go as a successful missionary and he did not have followers or friends at his disposal in all Galilean cities and among all classes of the people.

This is in accordance with the general impression we have drawn already from our sources, that the deeds and words of Jesus were *signs of the Kingdom of God*, nothing more and nothing less. Nothing more, for they do not introduce the Kingdom of Heaven on earth; and nothing less, for they are far more than advice and prescriptions for life during this age. In this statement we may find the key to the understanding of Jesus' entire mission. His miracles are a revelation of heavenly forces and a proclamation of what God is going to do. His decisions and commandments are meant to give evidence of the pure will of God. His entire personage is like a signal from heaven announcing that there is another world and that the other world is already moving toward this earthly world.

Regarding the Sermon on the Mount in the light of this conclusion, we have before us the solution of all the problems which we have faced up to this point. Our theory was that the commandments and the prophecies of the Sermon on the Mount are signs of the Heavenly Kingdom. Now we find a confirmation of this theory. When we interpret the sayings as signs we can understand and in some way reconcile the apparent contradiction which was till now implied in our consideration. On the one side we found that the Sermon on the Mount must be taken seriously as an expression of the divine will—even in this world. On the other side we recognized that the commandments of the Sermon on the Mount cannot be fully per-

formed in this age. The existence of God's demands
within this world as they are proclaimed in the Sermon
on the Mount is a sign of the Kingdom of Heaven,
judging us as well as blessing us. The radicalism of
the Sermon on the Mount is our judgment, its announcement of another world is our hope.

In the light of this conclusion we are able also to
understand the difference between the two halves of
the New Testament. What happened before Easter
was a series of occurrences on earth, which for faithful
men were signs of the coming Kingdom of Heaven.
After Easter all these events were interpreted as beginnings of the new world. For this reason, the Christian community preserved the tradition of the events;
but when Christians expressed their faith, they spoke
more of what the Lord was doing in their own midst
than of what he had been doing in the villages and
fields of Galilee. This is the reason for the difference
between the two halves of the New Testament.

As regards the sayings of the Sermon on the Mount
we may state that before Easter they were words of
Jesus spoken to reveal God's will, and that after
Easter these sayings were collected to be a rule of
conduct for the Christian communities. During his
lifetime the sayings of Jesus were intended to serve
as signs of the Kingdom of Heaven. Collected and
brought together in a slightly elaborated form in the
summary called the Sermon on the Mount, the sayings
became rules by which the Christians were to prepare
themselves for the membership in that Kingdom and

for a life "in Christ" meanwhile. Before Easter the simple words which we read in the Sermon on the Mount had more value than precepts of the sages, because the man who uttered them was a warrant of the Kingdom of Heaven, the personal embodiment of all faith and hope. His sayings were for his listeners judgment and a promise in the name of God. After Easter they became the law which the heavenly Lord has given. Now, however, the Lord has also given his Holy Spirit in order to strengthen his disciples and to fit them for a life according to the will of God, but within the limitations of an earthly existence.

This was the meaning of the Sermon on the Mount in the old days. For us who claim to be Christians in the present there is another question: what shall we do as Christians of today, if we want to be obedient to the Sermon on the Mount? This will be the last problem which we have to face.

CHAPTER VII

The Sermon on the Mount and the World of Today

IN THE preceding chapters we concerned ourselves with matters of a purely scientific, exegetical as well as historical, nature. We found it necessary to put aside all questions of today, all problems of our own century, in order to develop a clear understanding of the meaning of the biblical record. As a doctrine of Christian faith and of Christian ethics theology is seriously endangered by excessive haste in trying to draw practical conclusions. For this reason exegesis ought to be careful not to confuse the real problems of the Bible text with the questions of the present generation.

This holds good even for the Sermon on the Mount. Its commands concern many problems which appear to be questions of our daily life. Therefore every Christian reader who sees in the Sermon on the Mount more than an interesting document runs a risk of misunderstanding in the overhasty application of its rules to the problems of daily life, such as marriage, oaths, war and peace, economics. To avoid mistakes it was necessary first of all to consider the meaning of the Sermon on the Mount apart from the discussion of our modern problems, and to interpret first the meaning of the sayings of Jesus for his listeners and then the validity of the whole text for the first communities. Before we now turn to our own problems, we might well summarize once more the main results of our consideration.

(1) The Sermon on the Mount is composed of single sayings which Jesus spoke at various occasions to different people.

(2) These sayings were connected with each other to form a continuous discourse partly by Matthew, partly by the author of his source. In the source as well as in Matthew they provided a standard for Christian conduct within the Christian communities. Their use in this capacity represents a great change of function. Originally, when they were still isolated sayings, they served as a kind of prophetic sign, they proclaimed the Kingdom of Heaven, demanding a radically new attitude on the part of man. Combined to form a more or less complete system, the sayings in Matthew no longer proclaim a heavenly Kingdom; they describe a Christian life on earth.

(3) The consequence was the alteration of certain sayings. The words of Jesus proclaiming the law of the coming Kingdom were not fully applicable to the earthly conditions of the communities and therefore needed to be adapted to become usable.

(4) The Sermon on the Mount is not the only program of Christian conduct in the New Testament. The New Testament contains many other sayings of the same kind, especially the instructions for

the disciples, the well-known similes and parables and the admonitions found in the Epistles. But the Sermon on the Mount overshadows all of these and thus has special symbolic value as the great proclamation of the new righteousness. It soon became evident—to some extent even in the time of the ancient Church— that there is a gap between this ideal of Christian conduct and real life. At least, since the year 300 A.D. the members of the Christian Church lived under entirely different circumstances from those presupposed in the Sermon on the Mount. For this difference there are, it seems to me, two reasons.

The first reason is a change in the eschatological outlook. The Sermon on the Mount presupposes the belief that the world will come to an end. Therefore it no longer exists for the faithful man, who looks to heaven and is waiting for the coming salvation. On the other hand, the Church, after some decades of defeated hopes, came to the insight that it was its duty to cope with an enduring world, and to provide for centuries of existence. This was a radically different outlook which compelled the Christian communities to revise their ethics. Now the Church had not only to consider the questions of today and tomorrow and at the same time to trust that soon after tomorrow this world will come to an end. The Christians were rather compelled to pose the problem of a life "in Christ" within this world and its conditions, and to seek a solution of the tension between these conditions and the will of God.

The second reason for the difference between the apostolic age and the later period is that Christianity became responsible for this world. When certain Christians achieved high positions in the State, when rich and powerful men became Christians, the Church automatically ceased to be a sect separated from and protected against the course of this world. This development never reached a final conclusion in either direction, and that is what makes it a matter of such moment. The spirit of the world remained pagan, though the world was called a Christian world. The Church sacrificed its own ideals in part in order to incorporate the totality of human life, but it never fully succeeded in its efforts. The Church became the successor of the Roman Empire, it is true, but in so doing it forgot the word of the Lord: "My Kingdom is not of this world."

It was a consequence of this process of secularization, that the Church was more and more compelled to resign its old pretensions to sinlessness. The attitude of the apostolic age toward the question of sin in the Christian life is characterized by the word of Paul (Romans 8:3, 4): "God by sending His own Son . . . condemned sin in the flesh in order to secure the fulfilment of the law's requirements in our lives, as we live and move not by the flesh, but by the Spirit." But those Christians who, since the second century, had intercourse with the world were influenced by its tendencies, or as Paul would say, by the flesh. Repentance which had once been preached to the

pagan world became more and more necessary for the
Christian world as well. In the book of Hermas, the
so-called *Shepherd*, from the first half of the second
century, we read the proclamation of one single repentance and no more for Christians while the heathen
have a possibility of repentance and conversion till
the end of the world. During the third century repentance becomes a regular institution of the Church;
so urgent is the need that the Church must inevitably
concede that Christians are disobedient to the will of
God.

In spite of the sinfulness of its members the Church
claims to be holy. This claim is founded upon the conviction that the Church is a heavenly body; but this
body is not appointed to appear on earth during the
great eschatological catastrophe, which was the belief
of the first Christian generations. Rather the Church
is to penetrate humanity in the present and to take the
place of the Roman Empire. This is the great conception of the Church in Origen, and this view was enlarged and founded anew by Augustine. He has actually combined in his conception of the Church the
good qualities of the earthly and the heavenly Kingdom, and committed to the Church the great task of
the Roman Empire to establish peace on earth. He
has identified the Church and its hierarchy with the
Kingdom of Heaven, with the millennium, the reign
of a thousand years which the book of Revelation had
prophesied.

According to Augustine two worlds oppose each

other. They are no longer the pagan and the Christian world, for in the days of Augustine the Roman State had already become Christian. The two worlds are the earthly State and the heavenly Kingdom, *i.e.*, the State of God, the Church. The worldly State has to serve the Church; its greatest task, to bring peace, is to be performed by the Church, for the worldly State can preserve peace on earth only in a limited way. The peace of Babel is not a peace based upon the exercise of complete justice. Thus, the worldly State is of relative value, its rights and duties depending on the divine State.

This distinction between the earthly and the heavenly realm was of great importance for the Middle Ages. It seemed to be symbolized in the difference between the evil angels and the good angels as well as in the two sons of Adam, Cain and Abel. Consequently, the depreciation of the worldly realm was not a matter of recent development. It had been continued into the present, but only in a limited way. For, though assigned there to the lower of two levels, the earthly State had been given a recognized place in a unified scheme of things that included both the terrestrial and the heavenly Kingdoms. This was the natural consequence of the loss of eschatology.

The importance of this distinction for the problem of ethics cannot be overestimated. The heroic ideal of doing the radical will of God had to disappear on the lower level, for confronted with worldly problems it can assert itself only in combination with an eschato-

logical outlook. Man needs to be able to say: this world
will come to an end, its conditions will perish, the con-
tradictions of human life and its vexations will disappear—and then it *will* be possible for mankind to
perform the will of God in full. Today, this eschatological outlook is lost, at least practically so; it is
valid only in small, more or less heretical, circles, not
in the world of the renewed Roman Empire, *i.e.,* the
Church. Consequently, the ideal of full obedience to
God's will seems to be impracticable. The commandments of the Sermon on the Mount have no validity
for the workaday life, for the lower level of the Hier-
archic system. Therefore they must be replaced by
other rules. The most important theologian of the
Middle Ages, Thomas Aquinas, finds these rules in
the ethics of Aristotle.

These ethics are by no means orientated upon the
coming Kingdom of God. They have as their standard
the *agathon,* the good. Their ultimate aim as Aristotle
saw it was happiness on earth. In the Christian adap-
tation of these ethics made by Thomas the aim was
eternal happiness. To achieve it observance of the
praecepta, the basic rules of moral life, suffices. But
there are still other rules which demand more from
man, the so-called *consilia.* Those who want to be perfect must obey these *consilia* and must adapt themselves to the ideals of poverty, chastity and obedience.
The troublesome question how man can live in the
midst of this world and at the same time obey these
rules does not arise, because those who follow the

counsels (*consilia*) are to become monks. Thus the problems of a workaday life do not concern them. In this way, by dividing mankind into two classes, and ethical norms into the categories, mediæval theology was able to separate the problem of obedience to God's will from that of daily life. It assigned the more exacting demands to the higher class which is not troubled by worldly relationships.

The Reformation abolished the division between the two realms both in theory and in practice, but in a twofold manner. Lutheranism stated that this world is and for the moment remains sinful, but that God has called man to take part in its life. Hence man must serve God in doing his work in this world as loyally as possible and must trust in God's forgiveness, for it is impossible to become a saint in the midst of this world. In this way Lutheranism made man actually at home in this world and taught him to be even before God, what he had previously been only with a bad conscience, namely a good citizen of his State.

Calvinism on the other hand endeavoured originally to transform the world according to God's will and to create nations which want to become God's chosen people. This is the case where Calvinism controls the government of the State and dominates public life. Where this is impossible Calvinism creates a nucleus of good Christians in the midst of the world independent of and sometimes opposed to the worldly State.

In spite of this change in consequence of the Reformation, the secularization of this world gained ground more and more. Only small circles within the churches tried to live a real Christian life, but they did not influence the course of the world in a decisive way and were by no means responsible for this course. The mighty leaders of mankind were Christians by name, perhaps Christians in faith, but pagans in conduct, at least if we take the Sermon on the Mount as our standard.

The situation clarified itself in proportion as the world proceeded to rid itself more and more of the Christian spirit. This it has accomplished since the days of Rationalism and especially during the latter part of the nineteenth century. The development was that which we now call "Secularism," and which took in more and more of common life, especially in the field of politics. Christian principles henceforth no longer determined national policy. At some points in the development it seemed that philosophic or religious ideas might still be said to influence the national life of the world. But even in these periods those who looked deeper came to the conclusion that the governing forces in politics were actually power and money, ambition and, justifiably or not, national claims and pretensions to national expansion. The whole political development during the nineteenth century diverted the interest of men from their supernatural destiny and made them forget their transcendent ideals.

This is a well-known historical fact. But another contemporaneous development is often overlooked, at least in European theology. In the course of the nineteenth century not only new theoretical ideals but also a new style of life was developed, a consequence of the new methods employed in industry and business. Industry created a new type of man. His ideal was not to obey the commandments of the Bible or the Church or to live in accordance with philosophical doctrines. He was compelled to live with no more than the purpose of gaining his livelihood, of obtaining sufficient earnings, of outdoing his competitors and of achieving as much success as possible. While the process of secularization diverted people from their transcendent ideals, this process of mechanization all but abolished ideals entirely. This enormous transformation involved only certain classes of people among the civilized nations; but the great mass of people belonged to these classes. We all know the consequence of this struggle: impoverishment on the one side, capitalism on the other side, unchecked competition and class-war, conflict of interests and the apocalyptic plagues of our own era: war, revolution and unemployment!

This is the greatest failure of Christianity in modern times, that Christians have not been able to stop this development, to check this process, to overcome this crisis.

The reason for this failure is, in my opinion, first of all, that the Church was always so closely associated with the powers of this world that it did not venture to incite spiritual revolutions. The Sermon on the Mount is a storehouse of radical spiritual energy, but any one who might have dared to bring these forces to bear on civilization and on human conduct in the modern world would have appeared to be overthrowing the entire world, and this was what Christianity hesitated to do. Christianity was not revolutionary but rather conservative, some churches more so than others. Taken as a whole the churches of Christ functioned more as the good conscience of the world than as the bad. They preferred to support the order existing in this world rather than to criticize it, to strengthen the governing agencies rather than to oppose them. The Church, once the preacher of the eschatological Gospel, had become an enormously conservative power within this world.

In consequence of this attitude of the churches the new radical movements of the eighteenth and nineteenth centuries were antagonistic to the churches. Because they did not know anything about the radical forces of the New Testament, especially those of the Sermon on the Mount, these movements became opponents of Christianity as a whole. This holds for the French Revolution as well as for Marxism and Bolshevism. The Church in Europe seemed to be the bodyguard of despotism and of capitalism. For this reason all those who demanded that the condition of this world be improved were obliged to fight against Christianity. There were only a few solitary thinkers, whose knowledge of the Gospel was deeper and who recognized the radical power of the Christian message: *e.g.*, the philosopher *Sören Kierkegaard*,

Count Tolstoi and, in a sense, *Feodor Mikhailovich Dostoievsky.*

The Danish author *Sören Kierkegaard* (1813–55) was perhaps the first thinker who in the midst of the European "Christian" civilization fully realized the gap between the Gospel and human civilization. In strict opposition to the Hegelian philosophy he recognized the essential difference in quality between God and Man as the basic reason why Christ was compelled to suffer on earth. The Christian message does not improve the nature of man as the skill of a good equestrian improves the nature of a horse (to use Kierkegaard's own comparison). If God is to be really the teacher of man, his first lesson must be to subdue the disciple, for there is a tremendous antagonism between Christianity and all kinds of humanity, culture and education. Kierkegaard had discovered this antagonism not as an outcast of human society, as a member of a lower class or as a heretic who is opposed to the churchgoing people, but as an author of high qualities, as a well-educated man, and as a student of theology.

He recognized that the New Testament does not address man as a human being equipped with valuable natural gifts, but as a sinner, and only as a sinner. The New Testament conception of sin, however, is not the antithesis to virtue, as the traditional doctrine taught under the influence of Greek ethics had. The Christian views sin rather as the antithesis to faith, and therefore Christian preaching can come to men only as a paradox. It can be grasped only by suffering, the best example of which is Christ's fate on earth. Consequently to be a Christian does not mean to be honored for one's achievements. According to Kierkegaard this would be real paganism. The promise of a Christian life on earth is rather: if you do good, you will be punished!

Thus Kierkegaard came to the conclusion that Christendom has abolished Christianity by weakening the paradoxical character of the Gospel. It is easy to see that here in the middle of the nineteenth century a profound mind has rediscovered something of the true character of the Sermon on the Mount. The principal failure of the existing Christianity is in Kierkegaard's view the desire of the Christians to be established by God in their own worldly relationships. God here becomes a helper in the daily life, the Christian message was and is expected to bring comfort in all earthly troubles, and ministers are appointed to give the assurance of eternal happiness. But this is a humiliation of God and his revelation. It is impossible really to come into contact with God and at the same time to cling to human ideas of good and evil, whether comforting or disturbing. To Kierkegaard, this attitude seems to be Jewish rather than Christian.

Consequently Kierkegaard arrived at a very severe criticism of the existing Church. The Church (and especially an established Church) seems to be an instrument of quietism, and faith is an unquiet thing. About a distinguished Danish bishop he says: "Without doubt, he would not hesitate to die for Christ, in the case of necessity, but he takes care that the case of necessity does not occur." A real Christian faith, ready to sacrifice and to die, would be considered a strange thing in the eyes of the weak and indolent Christians of this time. This is how Kierkegaard repeatedly describes the contrast between the attitude of existing Christianity and early Christian radicalism, the best example of which is the Sermon on the Mount. He too feels it is not permissible thus glibly to abstract a law for this world from the sayings of the Sermon on the Mount. He is far from being a nomistic interpreter of the Gospel; it may be that this is a consequence of his Lutheran education. Kierkegaard knows that sometimes it is better to be a Christian than to do the so-called Christian deeds. In a very characteristic discussion between Eternity and a rich man he describes how Eternity asks whether the rich man during his life has been merciful. The rich man answers: "I have given hundreds of thousands for the poor." But Eternity is not satisfied by this answer, because to give something is not the same as to be merciful.

This is, without any doubt, a revival of early Christian radicalism; but it does not lead to a solution of the problem of a Christian life in the existing world. Kierkegaard rejects worldly means as suitable for organizing a Christian community. The Apostles did not discuss the possibility of making a complaint to the high court or of electing a synod. They knew

that Christians must suffer—and suffered. Kierkegaard does not see that the background of the primi-
tive Christian radicalism is an eschatological one. He
does not realize that in the meantime Christianity
must find a way to live in the existing world, perhaps an unchristian or half-christian world. At any
rate it is a world for which the Christians are no less
responsible than the unbelievers. Thus, in combination
with other elements of Kierkegaard's thought and of
his character, it is the loss of eschatology which prevents him from becoming a Christian leader or a
prophet and makes him an antagonist of existing Christianity.

At this point there is a resemblance between Kierkegaard and *Count Tolstoi* (1828–1910). The Russian
writer also preaches the uncompromising demand of
the Gospel, especially of the Sermon on the Mount,
but he is much more naïve as a thinker, often changes
his views and has for his criticism no theoretical starting point. Perhaps this vague and agnostic view is the
natural consequence of his education among the Russian nobility. Indeed, it is not his system but his
conduct which makes the whole personage of Count
Tolstoi so eminent that it is like a beacon in the
midst of the European crisis.

Count Tolstoi's view depends much more upon the
sayings of Jesus, especially in the Sermon on the
Mount, than Kierkegaard's. The Russian Count is
interested chiefly in ethics; theological questions in
the special sense of the word do not concern him. In

Tolstoi's opinion the Gospel is a summary of rules, radical but by no means impracticable rules. Its principal contents may be summarized in five commandments in accordance with the Sermon on the Mount: no anger, no divorce, no oaths, resist not evil, love your enemies. The most important and most characteristic of these commandments is the fourth: resist not evil. Consequently Tolstoi becomes the preacher of non-resistance in private as well as in public life. Those who consider these rules impracticable are men who want to find security in their earthly life. But—and there is a similarity here between Tolstoi and Kierkegaard—it is neither the intention of the Gospel to create security on earth nor the destiny of men to achieve security in their earthly life.

In this way Tolstoi recognizes the radicalism of the Sermon on the Mount and the revolutionary force of its rules. But he does not see their relation to the Kingdom of God in an eschatological sense. Consequently he puts the rules of the Sermon on the Mount in a wrong context, *i.e.*, in the life of this age. He attempts to change the whole course of this life, at least of his own life, in the direction of a static ideal formulated in accordance with the Sermon on the Mount. He does not see that Jesus himself referred to another world, to the Kingdom of God. He does not acknowledge his Messiahship but takes him simply as a teacher of this world. It is an unhistorical rationalistic way in which he interprets the Gospels; this interpretation springs out of the materialistic ideas of his own age and his education in a milieu where a scientific study of the Bible was lacking.

Furthermore, his attempt to establish a set of rules to govern the simple rural and uncivilized life on his estate in Yasnaya Polyana was not conditioned only by the New Testament. He was also influenced by a romantic spirit connected with his disgust for the life among the Russian nobility. He was full of compassion for his bondmen, but not full of love for his fellowmen, and his criticism of mankind and of the Church, of course his own Orthodox Church, was sometimes unjust and full of hate. He did not understand other ideas, and the tragedy of his life was that people did not understand him.

He himself expressed the consciousness of this tragic mistake in his posthumous drama, *Light Shining in Darkness*, which contains the most serious criticism of his own ideas. The principal person of this drama, Nikolai Ivanovitsch Sarynzev, intends to live according to the Sermon on the Mount, that is, without any property. He attempts to allow his peasants to steal the trees of his wood. He provokes the fiancé of his daughter to refuse military service, and a young orthodox priest to resign from his ministry. He tries to learn joinery and to gain his livelihood as a poor man. But he makes his family unhappy, and his friends accuse him of being a new Pharisee. The joiner, his teacher, regards his ideas as the foolishness of a nobleman, but he adds: "Why should I laugh at you? You pay me for my services." The unhappy preacher of a new world is unable to answer the question: what would be the fate of this world under his system? The drama thus gives impressive evidence of the experience that the Sermon on the Mount, taken in its radical sense, must remain impracticable in the world of today.

On the other side, Count Tolstoi has done much to awaken the social consciousness of his age by his writings as well as by his conduct. However, he did not fulfil his purpose, which was to improve living conditions in a wider circle outside of Yasnaya Polyana. Indeed, his personality was like a warning signal, but his attempts have to be considered as a social experiment without consequences for mankind.

The Russian writer *Dostoievsky* (1821–1881) testifies in another way to the radical power of the Christian message. He did not write philosophical pamphlets like the others, but spoke through the characters of his works. He recognizes the ambiguous character of man. He opens the darkest depth of the human soul and shows the demonic powers working there; the power which reveals the deepest things in man is suffering. Thus, Dostoievsky is convinced that the existing man is not the image of God. He is therefore in strong opposition to all kinds of humanitarian idealism and consequently to the feeling of bourgeois security, which was characteristic of the society during his lifetime. Man must be transformed and those who are fitted for such a transformation are not the well situated members of human society, but rather the

outcasts of all types. Indeed, some characters in Dostoievsky's novels seem to be impressive illustrations
of Christ's saying: "Verily, I say unto you, the publicans and harlots go into the Kingdom of God before you" (Matt. 21:31).

Consequently, Dostoievsky's view of this world has
an apocalyptic aspect. He recognizes the great alterna-
tives of this life: either man wants to be free and must
suffer or man prefers happiness—then he cannot be
free. The Church itself has chained him in order to
secure his life; it has chained him by miracle, mystery
and authority in analogy to the three offers of the
devil at Christ's temptation. This is the content of the
famous story of the Grand-Inquisitor and Christ in
Dostoievsky's novel *The Brothers Karamazov*. Christ
is the way to a new freedom, but freedom is not of
this world.

It is not the rigidness of the commandments in the
Sermon on the Mount which is illustrated in the
works of Dostoievsky. It is rather the radicalism of
the whole Christian concept which he depicts. The
principal idea in this concept is love without any bound-
ary, the illustration of which is the Staretz Sossima
in the novel mentioned above. Love compels man to
avoid the error of self-deification and to strive after
the ideal of God's incarnation in man.

In this way we recognize in the work of these thinkers, Kierkegaard, Tolstoi and Dostoievsky, three very
different attempts to give expression to the radical
forces of the Christian Gospel. These men were phi-

losophers and men of letters and as such unable to
lead or to influence the masses of men. Their readers,
men of the educated classes, were interested only in
the literary part of their work and did not hear their
message.

I do not wish to appear to disregard the enormous
results of the work of the Church in its own field during the nineteenth century. Christianity did not despair of its task. Foreign Missions, Home Missions
and all works of Christian charity gave clear evidence
of the survival of Christian spirit. But the Church
did not touch the masses. The new type of man, the
man who came into being during the great Industrial
Revolution, was and remained unshaken by the efforts of Christianity. Many of the leaders of the
working classes guided their followers far away from
every Christian attitude.

In this connection let me refer to another "voice
in the wilderness," a man who in an original and
inimitable way tried to express in his personal life
that connection between the Church and the working
classes which had been lost during the nineteenth
century. *Caspar René Gregory*, Professor of Theology at Leipzig, American by birth, German by fate,
born in 1846 at Philadelphia, killed in 1916 as an
officer in the German army, was professionally a great
scholar in textual criticism of the New Testament.
His life was devoted to the aid and assistance of people on every possible occasion, especially of the working classes. He wanted to make them feel the spirit of

Christian love—we may say: the spirit of the Sermon on the Mount.

Innumerable stories of such acts of assistance were told by the students of Leipzig University at the beginning of this century. There was the street-car switchman (they had no automatic switches in those days at Leipzig) who one evening stood at his post in the rain, cold and wet. Professor Gregory gave him some money and said "Go over to that coffee-shop and drink a hot cup of coffee." Then the professor took his place and carried on the work of a street-car switchman as long as the other was absent. Once he ran after a street-car to give an American stamp to the conductor because he knew that the man was a passionate stamp collector. And he too, like the nobleman in Tolstoi's drama, learned joinery, but not with the intention of renovating the world or of giving a good example; he wanted only to come nearer to his brothers of the working class.

And it was solely as the result of this point of view that he, aged sixty-eight, became a soldier in 1914. At that time he wrote in a letter: "My friends, the workmen, were compelled to join the army. It was intolerable for me, that they should say: 'Our friend, the Professor, has an easy life; goes to the University and we have to carry on war for him.' I wanted to stay with them in the rank and file and to share their pain of military life." The military service of Professor Gregory and his death by a shell hitting his quarters in France was indeed an illustration of the word: "Greater love has no man than this, that a man lay down his life for his friends." It was neither youthful enthusiasm which led him nor national hate; he wanted to be faithful unto death.

Since 1919 the situation has changed remarkably, at least in Europe. New ideas have come to expression, especially among the young men who had been soldiers in the war. New movements have arisen, based upon the distrust of the older generation and of their ideals. There are movements which endeavour to equalize the conditions of living, and other movements for more discipline within the nations and for a concentration of all national and racial powers. The general tendencies are in a sense socialistic: they do not acknowledge privileges of classes or nobility, they want to make as many men happy as possible, but they also want to make them able to render assistance to one another and to the groups to which they belong.

There is not only one such movement; there are many in different countries. The particular purposes to which they are dedicated vary and sometimes clash across the lines of national boundaries; but what is common is the tendency toward a better life for the masses, the trust in the gifts and powers of one's own nation, the enthusiasm for youth, the devotion to a leading personality, and the abandonment of the old ideals of quiet security.

These movements of the younger generation are partly in touch with Christian groups and partly op-

posed to the Christian faith. At any rate they do not
spring from and do not depend upon Christian ideals.
They have come into being without the influence of
Christian thought. In spite of this the churches dare
not neglect these movements, for the churches have
to do with the living generation and if this generation, especially the youth, is influenced in so large a
measure by these movements of national renovation,
the preachers of the Gospel must take some stand
with respect to them. Tensions are inevitable, for the
new spirit compels man to devote his life to his duties
within his nation, that is, to duties of this world; and
it sometimes happens that no time for other duties and
ideals remains. This may be called the most modern
form of secularization and a very serious one. It is a
real fervent enthusiasm which, on the side of the new
movements, enlists men's devotion and inspires him.
That is why the movements have achieved such astonishing results in the field of national recovery and of
social assistance for fellow countrymen.

It would be a great mistake on the part of the
churches if they were to be content merely to reject
and warn. They have rather to face the double problem of collaboration and of competition. The churches
have already made an attempt—of course only an attempt—to consider the matter. The Ecumenical Council for Life and Work held at Oxford 1937 discussed as
its main topic the problem "Church, Community and
State," the word "community" being used here in the
sense of national groups held together by a common

origin, a common spirit and common interests. But the problem cannot be solved by the discussions of a fortnight; its consideration must be continued in theory and above all in practice.

The difficulties confronting the Christian view of life and the maintenance of Christian ideals in the world of today are not determined by the appearance of new forces alone. There still exists the antagonism of the past, particularly the working man's distrust of Christianity and especially of the ideals of the Sermon on the Mount. Often tendencies of very different origin converge in the opposition against the application of Christian ideals to modern life.

The great mass of our contemporaries confronted with the Sermon on the Mount will merely shrug their shoulders. Most of them, even those who are radical opponents of the Christian Church and of Christianity, have the impression that the preacher on the Mount was a righteous and benevolent man, perhaps a Saint, but that his sermon is not applicable, not suited to the modern struggle for existence—in the field of economics as well as of politics. It seems to testify to the olden times, to a patriarchal ideal which no longer concerns us. These men, hearing the words, "blessed are the poor," would reply that that is not true; the cruel truth is that the poor man is damned in modern life. We as theologians bear in mind that the interpretation given by Matthew is right: "blessed are the poor in spirit," and we also know that poverty in the time of Jesus was a much

simpler thing than now. Consequently, the first be-
atitude does not glorify every poor man, definitely
not the proletarian of today, but the humble man who
is patient and waiting for the Kingdom of God. But
the man on the street does not know this. When he
reads the commandment to love one's enemy he
thinks: I need to love my fellow countrymen, my
fellows of the working classes and my family, but
why should I interest myself in my enemy? We have
recognized that the commandment to love one's
enemy is the most radical example of the general
commandment of love. We know that all the people
previously named, the fellow countrymen, the fellow workers, etc., are included in this general commandment. We know that love can be subject to no
restriction, when God is speaking to me through my
needy brother, whether he be friend or enemy. But
our man on the street does not know this and is probably altogether displeased by the commandment of
love. Confronted with the prohibition of cares he
would probably take it for granted that this commandment applies only to the wealthy classes, for
the life of the poor consists, and must consist, of cares.

We must realize that the man on the street—and
perhaps some others—have a similar reply for every
line of the Sermon on the Mount. Confronted with
these men we must acknowledge that not only the
war between the nations, but class war, competition
and the whole course of the modern life are in strict
opposition to the Christian ideal of the Sermon on

the Mount. All those who are entangled in this modern life are not prepared to hear the commandments of the Sermon on the Mount and to take them seriously because of their impracticability. Hence they want to be released from these commandments, for in the opinion of most of our contemporaries the commandments seem to be incapable of application, even in the greatest difficulties of our time, and therefore meaningless, at least in the great undertakings of economic, social and political life.

The worst thing is that Christian people also have no clear answer to this condemnation of Christianity. Most of them are conscious of the difficulties; many of them are trying to avoid the difficulties by adapting and interpreting the commandments—as did the Church from the very beginning. In Chapter IV I listed the best-known interpretations of Jesus' sayings, some of which claim to evade the difficulties rising from the severity of the Gospel. But because this severity is characteristic of the Gospel, it refutes such views, for they depend upon certain presuppositions.

It seems to me that we must also reject another interpretation. Some theologians are willing to confess that the commandments of the Sermon on the Mount surmount the capacities of men; but they suppose that this is the very purpose of the whole sermon. The disciples of Jesus are to be compelled to acknowledge their incapacity and sinfulness, but this deeper knowledge of their own nature is to lead them not into despair but to salvation through the crucified Lord, the warrant of forgiveness. Thus, the true understanding of human nature and its sinfulness would be the very aim of the Sermon on the Mount.

This interpretation seems to be in line with Paul's doctrine of the Law. For Paul it was the purpose of the Law and the effect of every one of its commandments to reveal sin as the mightiest power in human nature. But Paul's doctrine is formulated with reference to and determined by retrospect upon what has happened in history. He wants to make clear God's purpose in giving the Law: he wants to understand the paradoxical fate of Israel, God's chosen people, who, in spite of their glorious situation, lost their way and missed salvation. It was thoroughly clear to Paul that the same God who gave the Law also sent Christ to put an end to the Law, but the Apostle did not venture to make the statement that Christ's words were impracticable. For Christ's words are addressed to Christ's disciples; and the disciple—Paul says—can do all things through Christ who strengthens him.

Paul himself quotes some commandments of Christ in the First Epistle to the Corinthians, not in order to lead Christians to the cross, but to give them some rules for their common life. Therefore, to interpret the Sermon on the Mount as though it were only a way to the cross is not even genuinely Pauline. For Paul interprets Christian ethics more eschatologically and, thus, more optimistically than we do in the midst of our troubles and facing a more or less secularized Christianity. That is why Paul can say that he can do all things through Christ. Consequently, he takes all Christian commandments seriously as rules, not as negative references to the cross.

What is more, this interpretation, that the Sermon on the Mount must lead to the cross, is really incorrect, for the preacher on the Mount could not presuppose a foreknowledge of his death on the part of his hearers. Still less are they able to understand his death as a deliverance from sin. We are therefore obliged to seek another solution of our problem.

This solution, it seems to me, must be based upon the understanding of Jesus' words and deeds as *signs of God's Kingdom*. Jesus proclaims the pure will of God. He proclaims it by giving some radical examples of what God demands, but he does not describe the full application of God's demand to this world. This would be an impossible task, for the conditions of this world are not the conditions of God's work, God's Kingdom. A program for the improvement of this world would be applicable only to a community for a short period of time, because the conditions of our world are changing day by day.

There was already a difference in social order and conditions of life between the age of Jesus and the Middle Ages. There was a difference too in the days of the Lord between his native country and Italy. The more complicated the conditions of human existence became, the more rapidly the pattern of life has

changed and will change. The particular demands of
what we may call a Christian life depend upon the
political, economic, intellectual and emotional circumstances under which we live. The Christian must
live and act. What he needs is a standard and not a
description of his daily life. He looks on the New
Testament to discover not what precisely to do, but
how to act. And this holds good for the Sermon on
the Mount.

Jesus' commandments as well as his deeds are only
prophetic signs and those who want to be his disciples
must act in the same way as he did. They should be
ambassadors of God who proclaim His will by their
conduct. They should not be founders of a new Kingdom, because the coming of a new world depends upon
God's decision. The Kingdom is not yet present and
those who would undertake to found it in the midst of
this world would anticipate God's own decision.

By acknowledging this limitation imposed by our
own possibilities we are able to avoid grave mistakes.
To illustrate this let me tell a story from the life of
Friedrich Naumann, the German thinker and political leader, who died in 1919 as the head of the demo-
cratic party. He was formerly a pastor at Frankfort,
engaged in Mission work. In this earlier period he
was still inspired by the ideal of Christian socialism,
represented by Doctor Adolf Stoecker. In those days,
1899, Friedrich Naumann travelled through Palestine. He regarded the country with its memories in
the light of the conviction that it was the task of our

Lord to improve the present world through his deeds and words. This was then the conviction of the Christian Socialism in Germany, the representatives of which saw in the Gospel a social message. At this time Palestine was still governed by the Turks, and Doctor Naumann noticed the bad condition of the roads. Considering that during Jesus' lifetime these roads had probably been no better, he was very much disappointed. He was overwhelmed by crucial questions such as: did Jesus himself not notice the bad condition of the roads? And would he, in his love for mankind, not have been anxious to improve them? Or—was he in spite of his charity indifferent to the state of the roads? And did he remain so indifferent because he, as King of the coming world, made no claim to improve the conditions of this world? This was the starting point for Naumann's later development. He concluded that the Saviour, as God's ambassador, was not a reformer, and that therefore all those who want today to improve the circumstances of life are obliged to do this on their own responsibility before God. Thus, they would not be right in deriving a program of reform from the Sermon on the Mount.

To bring the matter into line with our considerations we must confess that the right answer to Doctor Naumann's question should have been as follows: Jesus did not actually claim to improve the condition of this world; his purpose was to proclaim the will of God, to point to the existence of His Kingdom by

words and deeds. When he pronounced commandments and rules, his purpose was not to improve the
world but to transform men. When he cured diseases
his purpose was not to renovate mankind but to give
some examples of God's grace. In this way he prophesied what God will do in the future by establishing
His Kingdom on earth. He, the healer, was a warrant
of this future. He gave to men a conviction of the
nearness of the Kingdom which stirred them and in
this way transformed them spiritually. This was all
that could be done in time before the end of the
world, namely to transform men in preparation for
the Kingdom and in this way to create a new type of
man: a man who is at home in the eternal world but
able and willing also to do his work on earth.

This is the meaning of all those deeds and words
in Jesus' life which I called the signs of the Kingdom.
They guarantee the existence of the eternal world and
its coming, and they give evidence of the new forces
revealed by the earthly appearance of Jesus and oper-
ating on earth in the present. The same situation
existed in the time after Easter. The first Christian
communities, also, were warrants of the Kingdom and
its coming, or, as Christians put it after Easter, they
were warrants of Christ and his coming. The Christian communities were witnesses to the new forces.
That is, they were witnesses to the Holy Spirit acting
in this world as the pledge and instrument of the
eternal world. It is true and will remain true that the
Sermon on the Mount claims to create a new type of

man and to bring together communities of such men as evidence of God's Kingdom within this world.

When we realize what kind of a world we are living in, we are obliged seriously to question whether it is still possible to give expression to the claims of the Sermon on the Mount today. No doubt, if we take the content of the Sermon on the Mount as an ideal of religion or of ethics, this ideal is remote from our modern life and will not and cannot be fulfilled on earth. But—as we have seen in the course of our analysis—the Sermon on the Mount is not an ideal but an *eschatological stimulus* intended to make men well acquainted with the pure will of God.

Whatever can we do with an eschatological admonition? We are not waiting for the end. We must needs be citizens of this world. We must provide for a life on the face of this earth. We have to live in the complicated circumstances of the modern age. It might seem that this gap between our world and Matthew 5–7 cannot be bridged over. What, then, about this message of the Sermon on the Mount in our days, what about its eschatological presuppositions?

(1) I shall speak first about the meaning of eschatology for our day. We do not think in eschatological terms today, and whatever may be the final fate of our world, we do not expect its end during our own life. But New Testament eschatology is more, far more than a presentiment of the imminence of the end of the world. It means that every pronouncement made in the books of the New Testament is made

from God's point of view. The Sermon on the Mount
does not speak of human or worldly conditions but
only of God's eternal will. We would misunderstand
the radicalism of this will, if we were to believe that
the Sermon on the Mount had been pronounced as a
body of instruction for this life, or as a program for
the reform of this world. Since the rationalism of the
eighteenth century we have been living in a period
of relativism. The ideals of our contemporaries in
politics and economics, in family life and in education are changing. Crisis follows crisis. Here in the
Sermon on the Mount we have before us, in the form
of pronouncements rather than in the form of
speeches, that is, in signs rather than in programs, a
declaration of the will of God quite independent of
our crucial situation. We are not able *to perform* it
in its full scope, but we are able *to be transformed
by it.*

(2) In spite of all differences between our time
and the days of Jesus we must stand for and uphold
this will of God if we believe in Christ as the Saviour.
The standard of the Sermon on the Mount and of the
Christian is not the trend—perhaps the noblest trend—
of our world, our time, our public opinion, for trends
are matters of passing moment in the history of the
world, sometimes matters of the next decades only.
The standard of the Sermon on the Mount and of
the Christian is the will of God. The basis of the
Christian attitude is the conviction that God's will
revealed in Christ's Gospel is the only hope for man-

kind. We must run the risk that only a few will recognize this will. Perhaps trouble will increase on this earth. Perhaps the world will withdraw still farther from the Gospel. We must risk this and we must wait. God does not reckon with decades but with centuries and with millenniums.

(3) The most important thing is that the Sermon on the Mount be effective in the hearts of Christians. We should not take it as a law in the Jewish sense, *i.e.*, we must not interpret it in a nomistic way, and thus perform literally what is written, and that alone, omitting what is not written. The Christian law does not demand of us that we *do something* but that we *be something*. In this way it creates the new type of man who knows the will of God and its ultimate eschatological aim, and who wants to live here and now in accordance with this will. But he accepts the conditions of this world as the inescapable basis of all his actions, and realizes that these conditions have completely changed since the days of our Lord.

This, then, is what the Sermon on the Mount demands—that Christians should live on their own responsibility before God. God's will comes to expression not in systems which are applicable only to certain periods and to certain parts of the world. God's will is revealed in our own midst by signs, the most perceptible of which are the sayings of the Sermon on the Mount. The conditions of this world are not amenable to the Kingdom of God and it is not our task to found this Kingdom. Rather our task is to perform signs, not the signs described in the Bible, but signs of our own time—to perform them as individuals, as communities, as churches, and if possible as nations. This would be the true fulfilment of Christ's promise: "He that believes on me, the works that I do shall he do also and greater works than these shall he do." The only presupposition here is the transformation of man. A community of men who by their belief and their conduct proclaim God's will is and would be the most convincing witness of God's Kingdom.

Many of us, Christians of all churches and countries, assume that the Sermon on the Mount should provide an answer to the actual questions of our day. It is for this reason that learned men, as well as men on the street, are intensively disputing the subject of these pages. If we bear constantly in mind the eschatological background of the Sermon on the Mount, we shall not be tempted to hand down ready-made decisions on the subject of these questions. The preacher on the Mount does not claim either to give a law or to construct a system of ethics. When he speaks, it is the world of God that is before his eyes and he does not regard the conditions of life on this earth, either those of his own time or those of the future. When he seems to decide some questions of this kind, for example, how to fulfil the Law or how to do justice, his purpose is not to reform legislation or the exercise of justice on this earth, but to illustrate the nature of God's will. For this reason we should not seek in the Sermon on the Mount authoritative decisions concerning questions of today, questions such as education, women's suffrage, the league of nations, nationalism, socialism, etc. Nobody will deny that problems like these concern our daily life; but it would be meaningless to seek an answer to these questions in the Sermon on the Mount. Even if Jesus would have discussed some of these problems he would have treated them as questions of his age and his country.

We may take as an example the attitude of Jesus toward the government. The highest political authority for his country during his lifetime was Cæsar, the Roman Emperor. But this was a foreign authority, a conqueror and, apart from all antagonism against the Roman methods, it is quite obvious that Jesus generally did not feel friendly toward this authority. The well-known word, "Render to Cæsar the things that are Cæsar's and to God the things that are God's," is not an expression of loyalty; its meaning is rather that the things of Cæsar do not concern the children of God; they must give tribute but without any feeling of loyalty. Probably the attitude of the apostle Paul toward the Roman government was different. He was not only a Roman citizen; he was above all a Christian missionary. In this function he may have appreciated the peaceful condition of the whole empire and the legal administration of the cities in the Roman provinces. It is not only the author of the Book of Acts who gives us this impression. This general attitude of the apostle is witnessed by the well-known admonition in Romans 13: "Every subject must obey the government authorities, for no authority exists apart from God." This attitude is in harmony with the situation of a missionary like Paul, who is always in conflict with the Jews and in some way protected by the Romans.

A generation later the situation had changed. Now the Roman government becomes more and more hostile toward the Christian communities. This antagonism grows till it reaches a great climax in the cruel persecutions under Decius and Domitian. With Constantine Christian rulers enter upon the scene and again the political situation of the Christians changes. Throughout the Middle Ages these rulers govern a more or less supranational empire. In modern times civilized nations live under national rulers who are responsible to their peoples. This has changed the relationship between rulers and citizens completely. What the rulers now demand is collaboration. There is no commandment in the New Testament which deals with collaboration with secular authorities. Therefore it is meaningless to seek specific commandments concerning these matters in the Sermon on the Mount.

We have, however, in the Sermon on the Mount a standard by which to solve such problems. All these questions of our daily life are to be decided by Christians as men who are responsible to God alone, and who know the pure will of God from the Gospel. Nobody can free Christians from this grave responsibility. Those who have been touched by the word of God are free to, but they are also bound to, give their decisions. Their liberty is based upon the conviction that there is no power in the world which can compel them. Their duty is grounded on the fact that the Gospel, because it is a Gospel of Love, will brook no negligence on the part of faithful men in these questions. The love of Christ constraineth us, as Paul says, and therefore Christians should tackle all these questions in the spirit of Christ, *i.e.*, according to the Sermon on the Mount. This does not mean an application of any individual sayings to the world of today. It means a continuous communication with God, whose will is recognized from the Sermon on the Mount.

When we try from this point of view to discover a Christian attitude to secular aims such as social uplift, friendship between nations and general cultural progress, we continually encounter one particular difficulty. The unchristian character of the world in which we live brings us face to face with an important question: should Christians co-operate in such matters of community enterprise even though they recognize that the guiding spirit of these undertakings is not Christian? Or should Christians withdraw from such enterprises and, if possible, establish separate Christian undertakings?

There is no single answer to these questions. Often for reasons of love Christians would do well to collaborate in the great common undertakings, for as community enterprises they have greater chances of success than the smaller undertakings of the churches. In this way Christians would be preaching the Gospel in a very impressive manner to those who must acknowledge that Christian people are the best collaborators ready to spend time, to give money and even to sacrifice themselves. But there may be other undertakings in which Christians cannot co-operate, lest they deny their discipleship. In such instances the most impressive proclamation of Christian spirit would be the foundation of a separate Christian undertaking, no matter how small. But on no account is it the duty of the Christian—according to the Sermon on the Mount—to limit his collaboration to expressly Christian enterprises. A Christian must recognize that the so-called Christian undertakings too are often under the influence of secular considerations or intentions, perhaps unconsciously so. At any rate, those who provide for matters of this world belong in some way to this world. This is the perpetual tension of the Christian life on earth. For it we have, while life endures, no other solution than the statement of St. Paul: "The life which I now live in the flesh I live by the faith of the Son of God who loved me and gave himself for me."

We began with a portion of the New Testament and are now concerned with the complicated problems of the modern world. This is the only correct procedure in trying to arrive at sound theological conclusions. In these days the whole of the Christian religion is being regarded with scepticism, and not merely parts of its history and doctrine as was the case in the last century. The question has arisen and will become more and more crucial as time goes on, whether Christianity is to remain as it was in the past, the principal religion of the majority of civilized nations, or whether the future will see the denial in principle of every Christian value.

I think that up to the present few of us have had any conception of what this means, either practically or otherwise. In the face of this danger a vague Christian idealism is insufficient as a basis for the witness we must bear. We must trace our convictions back to the Bible, the only common source of our faith. We need careful exegesis in accordance with the most modern methods of research, to help us understand what the Christian faith really is, and what the standards are which we as Christians seek to uphold in these times. It is at this point that the critical New Testament scholarship can serve the interests of the Christian religion in its struggle today.

INDEX

Abel, 109
Acts, 15, 33, 139
Adam, 109
Adultery, 57, 58, 67
Agathon, 110
Alexander the Great, 8
America, American, 2, 123, 124
Amos, 39
Apostles, 15, 29, 76, 117, 130, 139
Apostolische Quelle, 27
Aquinas, Thomas, 110
Aristotle, 110
Asclepius, 76
Athens, 33
Augustine, 108, 109
Authenticity, 6, 7, 31, 33, 43, 45, 46, 47, 62

Babel, 109
Bampton Lectures, 26
Basle, 27
Beatitudes, 15, 21, 22, 25, 26, 29, 31, 36, 38, 61, 62, 63, 127, 128
Beelzebub, 17
Benares, Sermon of, 40
Bible, 1, 7, 78, 104, 113, 120, 138, 143
Bolshevism, 114
Bousset, Wilhelm, 27
British Museum, 35
Brothers Karamazov, The, 122
Buddha, Buddhism, 40, 41

Cæsar, 55, 139
Cain, 109
Calvinism, 111
Christendom, 11
Christology, 8, 10, 78, 79, 80, 81, 87, 89, 90, 92, 93
Community, 126
Consilia, 110, 111

Constantine, 140
Corinth, Corinthians, 28, 29, 34, 43, 61, 89, 130
Corpus Hermeticum, 76

Danish, 115, 117
Decius, 140
Didache, 95
Divorce, 18, 28, 34, 59, 60, 61
Domitian, 140
Dostoievsky, 115, 121, 122

East, 3, 7, 48
Easter, 81, 82, 87, 89, 90, 102, 103, 134
Ecumenical Council, 126
Egypt, 35
Epistle, 9, 38, 89, 90, 91, 106, 130, 140
Eschatology, 8, 48, 49, 50, 52, 57, 60, 63, 64, 65, 71, 85, 91, 97, 98, 99, 106, 108, 109, 114, 118, 119, 130, 135, 137, 138
Eternity, 117
Eucharist, 29
Europe, 2, 113, 114, 115, 118, 125

Foreign Missions, 123
Formgeschichte or Form-criticism, 32, 42, 46, 69, 82
Fourth Gospel, 31, 37, 89, 90, 93
France, 124
Frankfort, 132
French Revolution, 114

Galilee, Galilean, 20, 79, 81, 90, 91, 100, 102
German, 12, 26, 27, 32, 80, 123
Germany, 27, 133
Golden Rule, 53, 72
Gospel of Love, 141
Gospel Tradition, 44, 92, 93

145

INDEX OF
SCRIPTURAL PASSAGES